D1003472

Adorno

Martin Jay

Harvard University Press
Cambridge, Massachusetts
1984

128298

Library of Congress Cataloging in Publication Data

Jay, Martin, 1944—
    Adorno.

    Bibliography: p.
    Includes index.
    1. Adorno, Theodor W., 1903–1969. 2. Sociologists—Germany
(West)—Biography. 3. Frankfurt school of sociology. I. Title.
HM22.G3A33 1984   193   [B]   84-3821
ISBN 0-674-00514-7

For Leo, our mutual friend

Contents

Acknowledgments

Susan Buck-Morss, Eugene Lunn, Richard Wolin and Lambert Zuidervaart, each of whom has written distinguished works on Adorno, have kindly read this book in manuscript. I have also benefited from the careful scrutiny of my wife, Catherine Gallagher, and the editor of this series, Frank Kermode. But my greatest debt is owed to Leo Lowenthal, to whom this book is affectionately dedicated. His friendship with Adorno began in 1921 and lasted for forty-eight years. Ours began in 1968, when I first started working on the Frankfurt School. May it last as long.

Introduction

'Wahr sind nur die Gedanken, die sich selber nicht verstehen.'[1]

THEODOR W. ADORNO

Adorno, let it be admitted at the outset, would have been appalled at a book of this kind devoted to him. The reason would not have been any reluctance on his part to assume the title of 'modern master'; excessive modesty was not one of his more noteworthy personal failings. Rather, Adorno would have had a principled objection to any attempt to render his thought painlessly accessible to a wide audience. True philosophy, he was fond of insisting, is the type of thinking that resists paraphrase. When his friend Siegfried Kracauer once complained of a feeling of dizziness produced by reading one of Adorno's works, he was testily told that only by absorbing all of them could the meaning of any one be genuinely grasped. Like the music of Arnold Schoenberg, which, so Adorno approvingly claimed, demanded of the listener 'not mere contemplation but praxis',[2] his own writing was deliberately designed to thwart an effortless reception by passive readers. In accordance with his dictum, 'the splinter in your eye is the best magnifying glass',[3] Adorno refused to present his complicated and nuanced ideas in simplified fashion. Charging the advocates of easy communicability with undermining the critical substance of what they claimed to communicate, he vigorously defied the imperative to reduce difficult thoughts into the conversational style of everyday language. What he once complained about in Heidegger could perhaps as a result

11

be extended to him as well: 'He lays around himself the taboo that any understanding of him would simultaneously be falsification.'[4]

Adorno, in fact, was highly suspicious of any attempt to extricate the content of ideas from the form of their presentation. The artistic side of his temperament bridled at the suggestion that thought could be reduced to a series of unequivocal and straightforward propositions unaffected by the mode and context of their expression. When an American publisher in 1949 balked at translating his *Philosophy of Modern Music* into English because it was 'badly organized'[5] and a well-meaning editor of an American journal recast one of Adorno's essays to clarify its argument, Adorno decided it was time to return to his native Germany. Not only would he escape the homogenizing tyranny of what he, and his collaborator Max Horkheimer, called the 'culture industry', but he also would be able once again to write entirely in German, a language which he claimed had 'a special elective affinity to philosophy and indeed to its speculative moment'.[6] His special brand of that tongue, which became known as 'Adorno *Deutsch*', was highly controversial, praised by some for its subtlety and flexibility, damned by others for what Karl Popper called 'simply talking trivialities in high-sounding language'.[7]

However one appraises it, Adorno's style stubbornly resists effective translation. The first courageous souls to attempt to render one of his books into English affixed a cautionary preface entitled 'Translating the Untranslatable'.[8] Since that initial effort, which was made in the mid-1960s, a number of other Adorno texts have been translated, although with somewhat uneven results. Perhaps significantly, in only a single case has a translator of one work been willing to try his or her hand on another.[9] Although, therefore, a selection of Adorno's writing is now available to English-speaking readers, it has been difficult to avoid the sense of missing something essential in our reception of his thought.

12

Introduction

Inevitable pangs of bad conscience must as a result accompany any attempt to capture Adorno in an introductory work of this kind written in a language other than German. Or at least they become inevitable once we take seriously his desire to resist the domestication of his ideas, rather than interpret it as merely a defence against making his actual arguments available for critical scrutiny or, what is perhaps worse, a weakness for what Arthur Lovejoy once called the metaphysical pathos of obscurity. Given Adorno's slashing critique of middle-brow culture's attempt to provide an instant veneer of sophistication – the 'familiar melodies from the great composers' syndrome – it is difficult to avoid feeling somewhat complicitous with the forces he sought so strenuously to subvert.

If, however, the paralysing effects of this guilt are to be at least in part overcome, two consolations suggest themselves. First, the now commonplace argument that the importance of texts is irreducible to the intentionality of their authors allows us to escape somewhat from the hold Adorno, like many other writers, wanted to exert over the reception of his work.[10] There are, we now know, inevitable impulses towards familiarization in the reading of all texts; we cannot fully escape the need to have them make sense *for us*. When we go one step further and try to rewrite them in another form, the effects of this process are intensified. To try to reproduce the original arguments in a manner wholly commensurate with their original style results in what looks more like a parody than a tribute, however it may be intended. Nor should we forget that those original texts come to us mediated by the intervening cultural space which includes previous interpretations and misinterpretations. If, as Adorno's friends Walter Benjamin and Leo Lowenthal liked to argue, the effects of a text, desired or not, are part of its meaning, then Adorno's 'work' now includes its historical impact. In a sense, then, even the commentaries that some may dismiss as mere primers for the fainthearted keep alive the energies unleashed by a creative intelligence.

13

Or more correctly, they contribute to that process if they fail to serve as complete surrogates for the original texts. The second justification for writing a study such as this is precisely the certainty of that failure. For however much skill or effort can be expended in trying to contain Adorno's achievement in so short a compass, its explosive power will surely burst through and make obvious to any reader the insufficiency of such an endeavour. It is, in fact, my hope that rather than foreclosing any further contact with Adorno's 'raw' texts, whether in German or translation, this exercise will persuade its readers of the value of addressing them directly. Although it is too much to ask, as Adorno did of Kracauer, to master his entire corpus – now in the process of being collected into twenty-three volumes by the Suhrkamp Verlag – the imperative to read his own words is especially powerful. For only then will the salutary inverse of this book's inevitable effect be achieved: that estrangement or defamiliarization of our own given ideas which results from any genuine encounter with an intellectual master, modern or otherwise. If our initial move towards domestication has an ultimate justification, it is, I would argue, only in the encouragement of that encounter.

Although, then, we cannot be entirely faithful to Adorno's thought and its mode of presentation, we can nonetheless suggest some of its richness by applying two of his favourite metaphors to his own intellectual career. In so doing, we may be able to convey some of the creative tensions within that career without resolving them into what Adorno once called, in reference to the literary criticisms of Georg Lukács, an 'extorted reconciliation'.[11] The first of these is the force-field (*Kraftfeld*), by which Adorno meant a relational interplay of attractions and aversions that constituted the dynamic, trans-mutational structure of a complex phenomenon. The second is the constellation, an astronomical term Adorno borrowed from Benjamin to signify a juxtaposed rather

14

than integrated cluster of changing elements that resist reduction to a common denominator, essential core, or generative first principle. In examining cultural and social phenomena, Adorno often used both metaphors to capture the subtle relations between and among their subjective and objective, particular and universal, historical and natural dimensions. The frequently remarked paratactic quality of his style,[12] with its refusal to subordinate arguments and observations in a hierarchically entailed manner, grew out of his unwillingness to privilege one element of the force-field or constellation over another. The result was not a relativistic chaos of unrelated factors, but a dialectical model of negations that simultaneously constructed and deconstructed patterns of a fluid reality. In ways that we will examine later, Adorno's dialectic was unremittingly hostile to the moment of triumphant reconciliation that traditionally capped a dialectical process. As he once put, 'The dialectic advances by ways of extremes, driving thoughts with the utmost consequentiality to the point where they turn back on themselves, instead of qualifying them.'[13] Accordingly, Adorno emphasized the critical role of exaggeration in cognition, exaggeration that brought into bold relief the tensions in a force-field or constellation rather than smoothed them over.

Were we to apply these metaphors to Adorno's own intellectual production, refusing to situate him squarely in one tradition, movement or school of thought, resisting the urge to qualify his extremes and modify his exaggerations, the following pattern would emerge. The map of Adorno's own constellation, the diagram of his own force-field, would contain five primary points of light and energy.

The brightest star in his constellation, to begin with, would be that of Marxism, or more precisely the heterodox tradition of Western Marxist thought inaugurated by Georg Lukács and Karl Korsch in the years immediately following the First World War. Adorno is commonly and correctly understood to have been a leading member of one of Western Marxism's most creative contingents, the so-called 'Frankfurt School' that comprised the inner core of the Institute of Social Research founded in that city in 1923. Along with Max Horkheimer, Herbert Marcuse, Friedrich Pollock and Leo Lowenthal, Adorno was a major architect of the School's Critical Theory, which in important ways both continued and subtly undermined the Hegelian Marxism of Lukács and Korsch. As its name implied, Critical Theory drew far more sustenance from the tradition of critique in Marxism than from its competing scientific impulse. It understood and defended the debt Marxism owed to classical German philosophy, even if it stressed the extent to which Marxism went beyond it.

Like virtually all other Western Marxists, Adorno was an uncompromising intellectual, who found no successful way to link his theory with the politics of the proletariat or any other radical social force. Nor was he willing to submit himself to the discipline of one of the parties claiming to speak for the oppressed. Scorning calls for solidarity by more orthodox Marxists, he stubbornly defended the virtues of what he called '*nicht mitmachen*', not playing along or compromising in the name of practical expediency. His refusal to compromise grew out of a characteristically Western Marxist insistence on the utopian potential of modern society, which prevented him from ever confusing any actually existing socialist regime with the genuine realization of the socialist dream. Adorno's intransigence on these matters meant that he represented in quintessential form the independence – and the isolation – so characteristic of Western Marxist intellectuals.

The next most powerful force in his field would be that of aesthetic modernism. In addition to his talents as a philosopher and sociologist, Adorno was a serious musician and composer, deeply indebted to the revolutionary atonal techniques he had absorbed from the Schoenberg school of modern music in Vienna during the 1920s. Not only did he write extensively about virtually all facets of music, both classical and popular, but his 'atonal' style of writing, indeed of thought, was itself affected by the compositional principles he had mastered in his youth. Although Adorno was not uniformly impressed by all currents of aesthetic modernism, as is evidenced by his running quarrel with Benjamin over Surrealism, he remained a staunch supporter of modern art against any calls for a return to classical or realistic alternatives. Other Western Marxists like Louis Althusser, Ernst Bloch and Galvano Della Volpe may also have championed modernism, but Adorno was the only one who could legitimately lay claim to have been a modernist himself. Not surprisingly, his work culminated in a massive study of *Aesthetic Theory* left still uncompleted at his death in 1969. Over it hovered the figure of Samuel Beckett, the most uncompromisingly modernist writer of the postwar era, to whom Adorno had intended to dedicate the book.[14]

All the more surprising then is the third star in his constellation, that of mandarin cultural conservatism. Adorno, despite his Marxist and modernist inclinations, cannot be fully understood without reference to the often regressively oriented romantic anti-capitalism of pre-First World War Germany. His visceral distaste for mass culture, unrelieved hostility towards bureaucratic domination, and untempered aversion to technological, instrumental reason were all earmarks of a consciousness formed in the wake of what has been called the decline of the German mandarins.[15] So too was the deep current of pessimism that informed his thinking, even as he insisted on the importance of maintaining utopian hopes. His controversial and highly nuanced appreciation of Spengler and other ostensibly reactionary figures testified to his desire to rescue what remained of value in the romantic critique of modernization.[16] Adorno's impassioned rejection of concrete political practice likewise betokened a mandarin sensibility classically expressed in his friend Thomas Mann's *Considerations of an Unpolitical Man*. It

17

naturally led to the reproach of more activist leftists that he was an elitist who betrayed the political implications of his own work, a reproach best typified by Lukács's celebrated charge that Adorno had 'taken up residence in the "Grand Hotel Abyss"'.[17]

Mentioning Lukács, however, reminds us that the roots of Western Marxism were themselves watered by many of the same impulses that produced the Spenglers and Manns of German culture. As Michael Löwy has demonstrated,[18] there was also a left-wing potential in romantic anti-capitalism that explains many early Western Marxists like Bloch, Benjamin, Marcuse and even Lukács himself. Adorno, in fact, consciously struggled to turn the arguments of mandarin cultural despair in an ultimately positive direction. 'Not the least among the tasks now confronting thought', he insisted, 'is that of placing all of the reactionary arguments against Western culture in the service of progressive enlightenment.'[19] Thus, for example, he often implicitly drew on the typical mandarin distinction between culture and civilization, but at the same time warned against the fetishistic hypostatization of *Kultur* as a realm of pure values above society. However much he may have distinguished between high and mass culture, he never forgot that 'all culture shares the guilt of society'.[20] Nor did he allow himself to feel that nostalgia for lost communities (those organic *Gemeinschaften* Ferdinand Tönnies had contrasted to soulless modern *Gesellschaften* or societies) which animated so many of his contemporaries, even if at times he did seem to yearn for the return of the presumably authentic individuals of early bourgeois culture.

Not only did Adorno distance himself from regressive fantasies of organic wholeness in the past, he also profoundly rejected all attempts to posit any new ones in the present. The materialist in him balked at the domination of objective otherness implied in idealist dreams of a fully constitutive meta-subjectivity. Nor was he impressed with the claims of thinkers like Martin Heidegger to have

18

located a realm of Being prior to the split between subject and object. In fact, unlike most mandarins, he took seriously the demands for personal, corporeal gratification revealed by the psychoanalysis whose insights he sought to incorporate into his version of Critical Theory.

It was perhaps the countervailing pull of a fourth force in Adorno's field, the muted but nonetheless palpable Jewish impulse in his thought, that prevented him from ever fully embracing mandarin values. Adorno, to be sure, was not as deeply involved with Judaism as Walter Benjamin, whose friendship with the great scholar of the Kabbalah, Gershom Scholem, had a profound impact on his thought. Nor was Adorno, only half-Jewish by birth, quick to identify with his father's co-religionists during the Weimar era. In fact, he even briefly toyed with embracing his mother's Catholicism, the faith into which he had actually been baptized, although like most leftist intellectuals of the time, his cosmopolitanism precluded any sectarian, ethnic or religious identification.

During his exile from Nazi Germany, however, and even more strongly in the years after the full extent of the Holocaust became known, Adorno came to acknowledge the true ramifications of his Jewish heritage. The implications of Auschwitz, in fact, became almost an obsession with him, especially after his final return in 1953 to a Germany unwilling to confront and work through its 'unmastered past'.[21] In one of his most frequently cited remarks, he insisted that, 'To write poetry after Auschwitz is barbaric.'[22] Indeed, the horrors of the death camps confirmed for him the truth of Brecht's bitter claim that the mansion of culture was built on dogshit. As late as 1966, Adorno would still muse with all the torment of the survivor on the question

whether after Auschwitz you can go on living – especially whether one who escaped by accident, one who by rights should have been killed, may go on living. His mere survival calls for the coldness, the basic

19

principle of bourgeois subjectivity, without which there could have been no Auschwitz; this is the drastic guilt of him who was spared.[23]

In more substantive terms, the Jewish star in Adorno's constellation meant several things. Like Horkheimer, he justified his refusal to spell out the utopian alternative to present-day society by reference to the Jewish prohibition on picturing God or paradise. That he nonetheless held to the belief in the possibility of achieving that utopia – or more precisely put, in the value of such a belief, whether it be plausible or not – was evidenced in his assertion that

> The only philosophy which can be responsibly practised in face of despair is the attempt to contemplate all things as they would present themselves from the standpoint of redemption. Knowledge has no light but that shed on the world by redemption: all else is reconstruction, mere technique. Perspectives must be fashioned that displace and estrange the world, reveal it to be, with its rifts and crevices, as indigent and distorted as it will appear one day in the messianic light.[24]

The messianic light cast by the Jewish 'star of redemption', to borrow the title of Franz Rosenzweig's famous book, a book which in fact may have indirectly influenced Adorno,[25] would not, however, shine one day on another world of flawless unity, a perfectly realized plenitude of the type extolled by Hegelian Marxists like Lukács. Instead, it would illuminate a landscape of benignly interacting particularities each individually different from the rest. The major lesson Adorno drew from the Holocaust was, in fact, the link between anti-Semitism and totalistic thinking. The Jew, he now came to understand, was regarded as the most stubborn repository of that otherness, difference and non-identity which twentieth-century totalitarianism had sought to liquidate. 'Auschwitz', he grimly concluded, 'confirmed the philosopheme of pure identity as death.'[26]

Adorno's identification of life with non-identity, a concept whose full ramifications we will explore later, also expressed what might be seen as the fifth and final force in his field. Its power can be grasped only if we bear in mind the injunction to include the historical afterlife of a work in our account of its significance. This star goes by the name of deconstructionism, the movement which recently emerged from the writings of post-structuralist thinkers in France to seduce or scandalize a large part of the Western intellectual world. Adorno, of course, died at virtually the moment that deconstructionism was born in the remarkable year of 1967,[27] but as one commentator has correctly noted,

The parallels between deconstruction and Adorno are particularly striking. Long before the current fashion, Adorno was insisting on the power of those heterogeneous fragments that slip through the conceptual net, rejecting all philosophy of identity, refusing class consciousness as objectionably 'positive', and denying the intentionality of signification. Indeed there is hardly a theme in contemporary deconstruction that is not richly elaborated in his work . . .[28]

The links between Adorno and post-structuralism extend, in fact, beyond merely fortuitous parallels, for in the figure of Walter Benjamin a more historical connection can be discerned. During his exile in Paris in the 1930s, Benjamin was known to the circle of proto-deconstructionists at the Collège de Sociologie, led by Georges Bataille, Pierre Klossowski, Roger Caillois and Michel Leiris, who seemed to have shared certain of his concerns.[29] Benjamin's important theory of allegory, which was crucial for Adorno's development, also had echoes in deconstructionism, shorn, to be sure, of its redemptive moment. Not surprisingly, Jacques Derrida himself wrote a positive essay on Benjamin, which implicitly acknowledged the subtle parallels in their thought (and by extension his and Adorno's).[30]

21

In Adorno's case, the clinching argument demonstrating his anticipation of deconstructionism derives from their common appreciation of Nietzsche.[31] Unlike many other Marxists who followed Lukács's lead in condemning Nietzsche as a dangerously irrational precursor of fascism, Adorno honoured him for his trenchant critique of mass culture and politics, his ruthless exposure of the bankruptcy of traditional metaphysics, and his penetrating insight into the ambiguous dialectic of the enlightenment. It was with the facile dismissal of Nietzsche in mind that he wrote, 'Thought honours itself by defending what is damned as nihilism.'[32] Although there were many aspects of Nietzsche that the Marxist in Adorno disliked, and although the pessimistic cultural mandarin in him led to his defence of a 'melancholy' rather than 'gay science',[33] he was always drawn to the explosively critical energies of Nietzsche's thought. And concomitantly, while never as trapped in 'the prison-house of language' as some of Nietzsche's contemporary French disciples, or as contemptuous of the search for truth, he in many ways anticipated their positions. As Michel Foucault has acknowledged,[34] there are striking parallels between his own analysis of the disciplinary, carceral society of modernity and Adorno's 'administered world'.

The force-field of Adorno's intellectual career, as it appears to us now, would thus include the generating energies of Western Marxism, aesthetic modernism, mandarin cultural despair, and Jewish self-identification, as well as the more anticipatory pull of deconstructionism. Although at certain moments and in certain moods Adorno may have been attracted more to one of these poles than to another, his work as a whole can best be grasped as an uneasy tension among all of them. It is thus misleading to argue, as have some commentators, that he was *really* a mandarin pretending to be a Marxist or simply a deconstructionist *avant la lettre*. We must rather, in a way that is more in accord with the deepest impulses of his own approach, understand him as the shifting nodal point

22

in which all intersect. Adorno often spoke out for the value of particularized individualism, but he was always enough of a dialectician to recognize that individuals are constituted out of overlapping and often conflicting relational contexts. To reveal as best we can the unique phenomenon that was Adorno, we must therefore conceptualize him in a manner which will be as true to the unresolved tensions in his thought as possible, rather than seek to find some putative coherence underlying them.

Indeed, within each of the 'forces' or 'stars' mentioned above, and one might add others like psychoanalysis, it would be possible to discern still subtler contesting impulses that would help us to get Adorno into better focus. But rather than pursue this refinement of Adorno's constellation, situating him in an ever more particularized field of countervailing energies, it is time to turn our instruments in a different direction and present Adorno more in his own terms. After a brief account of his life, we will attempt to spell out the philosophical underpinnings of his work and then investigate the ways in which they influenced his analyses of social, psychological and cultural issues.

1. A Damaged Life

'Das Leben lebt nicht.'[1]
FERDINAND KÜRNBERGER

There is a well-known photograph of Adorno, often used by the Suhrkamp Verlag in the promotion of his books, that strikingly expresses his personality, indeed his life-history. Taken when he was in late middle age, it shows Adorno in profile facing to the left, with a harsh light illuminating only the front part of his head and the outline of an ear. Cropped about two inches above his brows, the photo concentrates our attention on the mournful expression on his face. His lips are downcast, slightly, almost imperceptibly open, and apparently dry. The one eye we see is hooded, with its gaze directed inward; the backwards tilt of his head suggests someone lost in his own unhappy thoughts. The glasses he sometimes wore in other pictures are absent; totally self-absorbed, he allows no returning look. The cumulative effect produced by the photo is powerful, showing us a man brooding in subdued sadness about the untold horrors of his lifetime. Adorno's 'melancholy science', the result of his 'reflections from damaged life', is here itself reflected in the image of his face. The social physiognomy he tried so painstakingly to interpret is mirrored in his own individual countenance. As he once wrote of Samuel Beckett, 'No amount of weeping melts the armour; only the face remains on which the tears have dried up.'[2]

The auguries for so bleak an outcome were not very clear when Theodor Ludwig Wiesengrund was born in Frankfurt am Main on 11 September 1903. He was the

24

only child of a wealthy and assimilated Jewish wine merchant, Oskar Wiesengrund, and his Catholic wife, Maria Calvelli-Adorno, of Corsican and originally Genoese descent. The young 'Teddie's' early home life was comfortably sheltered, both economically and culturally, in the way that only an upper-bourgeois, European child's could be in the years before the First World War. From all accounts, his childhood provided him a model of happiness whose memory served as a standard against which he would measure all subsequent disappointments. Although his father may have been a somewhat distant figure, his mother, who bore him when she was thirty-seven, seems to have showered him with the attention that a child arriving late in life often receives. Along with her unmarried sister Agathe, who lived with the family, she instilled in him an early and lasting fascination with music. The Calvelli-Adorno sisters were in fact accomplished performers, the mother as a professional singer and the aunt as a pianist with the talent to accompany the celebrated soprano Adelina Patti at many of her recitals. Adorno was himself trained in piano by Bernhard Sekles, who also taught Paul Hindemith, and many years later still possessed the skill to impress Thomas Mann very deeply with his playing of Beethoven's difficult Sonata Opus 111.

Precocious musically and intellectually, Adorno was encouraged to develop his gifts in both directions. At the age of fifteen, he was introduced to German classical philosophy by a friend of the family, Siegfried Kracauer, fourteen years his senior, with whom he began a weekly habit of reading Kant's first *Critique*. From Kracauer, who was soon to become one of Weimar's most noted cultural critics and a major theoretician of film, he learned to decode philosophical texts as documents of historical and social truth. He also became sensitive to the subtle expressions of material, human suffering submerged in such writings, those irreducible cries of pain that idealist systems vainly sought, theodicy-like, to transfigure.

Adorno

Although in later years Adorno's friendship with Kracauer had its tensions,[3] his early debt to his mentor's anti-idealist, micrological culture criticism would remain potent throughout his life.

In 1921, Adorno graduated from the Kaiser Wilhelm Gymnasium in Frankfurt and enrolled in the city's newly founded and in many ways progressive Johann Wolfgang Goethe University. Already the author of two published articles, the first on Expressionism and the second on an opera by his piano teacher,[4] he devoured courses in philosophy, sociology, psychology and music to emerge with a doctorate in philosophy only three years later in 1924 at the age of twenty-one. His dissertation was written under the direction of an unorthodox neo-Kantian with strong artistic interests of his own, Hans Cornelius, whose early attraction to the empirio-criticism of Mach and Avenarius had earned him the attention (and the hostility) of no less a defender of materialism than Lenin. Cornelius was, however, also a man of the left, if more of the non-materialist variety that flourished in the Weimar Republic than of its Marxist competitor. Adorno, whose political sympathies were still inchoate, had no difficulty ignoring Lenin's strictures and working with Cornelius on his dissertation, which was devoted to the then fashionable phenomenology of Edmund Husserl.[5]

Nor did another young philosopher, Max Horkheimer, whom Adorno met in one of Cornelius's seminars on Husserl in 1922. From a background no less gilded than Adorno's – his father was a wealthy Jewish textile manufacturer from Stuttgart – Horkheimer had been drawn to the ethically charged libertarian socialism that attracted so many bourgeois sons in the aftermath of the war. The author of several unpublished novellas,[6] he also shared many of the same aesthetic interests as Adorno. And like his new friend, he was fascinated by psychology, initially in the form of the Gestaltism promoted by their common teacher Adhémar Gelb, and then in that of psychoanalysis. Although Horkheimer was eight years older than

26

Adorno, they began a friendship that soon turned into an intense intellectual collaboration which lasted for nearly a half century. Few such partnerships were as fertile and productive in this century as theirs.

Shortly before his graduation from the university, Adorno attended a performance of excerpts from Alban Berg's new opera *Wozzeck*, whose extraordinary power he immediately recognized. Through a mutual friend who had conducted the work, he arranged a meeting with Berg and persuaded the composer to accept him as a student in Vienna. Arriving in January 1925, Adorno soon entered the circle of innovative composers around Arnold Schoenberg, whose controversial 'new music' was then already leaving behind its atonal phase for the serialism of the twelve-tone row. Adorno was especially sympathetic to the earlier 'expressionism' of Schoenberg and his followers, which he discussed and defended throughout his life in a flood of essays and books that began with contributions to the Viennese journals *Anbruch* and *Pult und Taktstock*. Stressing music's cognitive rather than expressive dimension, Adorno did not, however, interpret expressionist atonality as the product of its composer's emotional subjectivity. Instead, he understood it in terms of the development of objectively immanent tendencies in music itself, tendencies which in complicated and indirect ways could be related to social trends as well. In a later essay written for Schoenberg's sixtieth birthday entitled 'The Dialectical Composer',[7] Adorno praised him for negating the bourgeois principle of tonality and exposing its claims to naturalness in the same way that dialectical thought undermined the pseudo-naturalism of bourgeois economics.

Adorno's interpretation of the 'new music' in these philosophically laden terms seems not, however, to have endeared him to his teachers in Vienna. This 'somewhat overly articulate youth',[8] as his friend Ernst Krenek later called him, was too theoretically and politically self-conscious for his more narrowly musical mentors;

27

even Berg, so Adorno later admitted, found his brutish seriousness a source of some irritation. In 1927, Adorno returned to Frankfurt to resume his scholarly studies. His ties to Vienna were not, however, severed, as demonstrated by his editorship of *Anbruch* from 1928 to 1932. As an actual composer, Adorno may have ultimately been unsuccessful,[9] but the musical training he acquired in Vienna had a profound effect on all his later work, not only as a cultural *point d'appui* but also as a model for his theoretical method. As many later commentators noted, his was an 'atonal' philosophy deeply indebted to the compositional techniques of the Schoenberg school. He was profoundly impressed in particular by Schoenberg's insistence on the truth content of his music, an insistence that found its linguistic equivalent in the theories of the other major presence in Adorno's Vienna, Karl Kraus.

The intellectual milieu to which the twenty-four-year-old Adorno returned after his Viennese interlude was much broader than the university community *per se*. His friendship with Horkheimer brought him into loose contact with the newly founded Institute of Social Research, then under the direction of the Austro-Marxist historian of the labour movement, Carl Grünberg. Through Kracauer, he had already met in 1921 and begun a lifelong friendship with one of its other members, the sociologist of literature, Leo Lowenthal. Although Adorno did not actually publish anything for the Institute until 1932, when he contributed an essay on 'The Social Situation of Music' to the inaugural issue of its journal, the *Zeitschrift für Sozialforschung*,[10] he was already in its intellectual orbit by the late 1920s. At about the same time, his circle of friends widened to include a group of heterodox Marxists, then in Berlin, which comprised Ernst Bloch, Bertolt Brecht, Kurt Weill and, most important of all, Walter Benjamin. Adorno's writings during these years began to show evidence of his newly acquired Marxist sympathies, which in fact had been initially stimulated earlier in the decade when he read Bloch's *Spirit of Utopia* and Georg

Lukács's *History and Class Consciousness*. Although always keeping a certain distance from his friends' more activist politics, especially when they defended the Soviet Union and the German Communist Party, Adorno began to practise a kind of immanent critique of ideology that was clearly indebted to the Hegelian reading of Marx contained in many of their works. Here too there was a bond with Horkheimer, whose philosophical inclinations, despite a certain sympathy for Schopenhauer, ran in the same direction. Although Adorno's commitment to Hegelian Marxism was never as unequivocal as that of a subsequent Institute colleague, Herbert Marcuse, whose enthusiasm for the newly discovered early manuscripts of Marx Adorno seems not to have entirely shared, his work clearly bore its stamp from the late 1920s onward.

The first explicit expression of his new orientation came in his unsuccessful *Habilitationsschrift* of 1927, 'The Concept of the Unconscious in the Transcendental Theory of Mind'.[11] Written for Cornelius, it attempted to find compatibilities not only between his teacher's heterodox neo-Kantianism and Marxism, but also between them and another highly controversial theory, the psychoanalysis of Sigmund Freud. Although Adorno had been exposed to Gestaltism during his earlier Frankfurt days, he had come to know Freud's work only during his years in Vienna or possibly on his subsequent trips to Berlin. As had been the case with his interpretation of Schoenberg's music, he stressed its cognitive implications, as a method for making the contents of the unconscious available for rational consideration. Not surprisingly, Cornelius was sceptical of the project, whose Marxist conclusions seemed particularly gratuitous, and Adorno was forced to turn to another topic to gain his *venia legendi* (right to teach at the university level).

His new subject was the then recently rediscovered philosophy of Søren Kierkegaard, which was particularly influential in the circles around the most prominent young philosopher of the Weimar Republic, Martin Heidegger.

Adorno's critique of Kierkegaard, nominally sponsored by the theologian Paul Tillich because Cornelius had left the university to emigrate to Finland, was entitled *Kierkegaard: Construction of the Aesthetic.*[12] It was the first of Adorno's many critical analyses of existentialism, whose questionable political implications he was among the earliest to recognize. Challenging Kierkegaard's defence of subjective immediacy against Hegel's alleged annihilation of it in the name of an all-encompassing rational system, Adorno demonstrated the abstractly one-sided nature of a subjective particularism that extracted man from his concrete historical setting. Kierkegaard's realm of spiritual inwardness, he argued, was itself an ideological reflection of the interior of nineteenth-century bourgeois homes, which purported to offer a refuge from an increasingly unpleasant external world. Although Kierkegaard had been anxious to debunk Hegel's idealist identity theory, in which subjects and objects were assumed to be one, he actually provided a pseudo-reconciliation of real social contradictions by giving ontological significance only to the spiritualized subject. This unwarranted reconciliation thus also produced an identity theory despite itself, because it posited an object-less dialectic of pure subjectivity.

Anticipating his later stress on the cognitive power of art, Adorno chastised Kierkegaard for denigrating the aesthetic stage of development as inferior to the ethical or religious. Whereas Kierkegaard argued for that inferiority because an aesthetic consciousness was still tainted by sensual and material concerns, Adorno praised it precisely for its mixed status, which provided more accurate knowledge of the still unreconciled contradictions of the real world. What Kierkegaard had attacked for reflecting man's 'creaturely immediacy' was thus truer to the historical circumstances of the modern age, which the Danish philosopher had sought to escape rather than change.

Accepted for Adorno's *Habilitation,* his study of Kierkegaard was published on the fateful day in 1933 when Hitler came to power. It thus had little immediate impact in Germany, as was also the case with the important address Adorno delivered in May 1931 when he assumed his teaching position in philosophy at the University of Frankfurt. The lecture, entitled 'The Actuality of Philosophy',[13] was in fact never published during Adorno's lifetime, but provided an early statement of the approach that Adorno was to use in most of his subsequent work. It demonstrated in particular his debt to the idiosyncratic philosophy of Walter Benjamin, which had deeply impressed Adorno when he read his friend's *Origin of German Tragic Drama* in 1928. In complicated ways, Benjamin's impact was also apparent in another significant talk Adorno gave in the waning years of Weimar, 'The Idea of Natural History'.[14] Here too publication would have to await Adorno's death, but many of its points were incorporated in his later work, most obviously in his 1966 *magnum opus*, *Negative Dialectics*. Although there were of course certain nuanced changes of emphasis in Adorno's position over the years, its essential continuity is demonstrated in the anticipations these early talks, written before his thirtieth birthday, contain of his mature work.

With the Nazi seizure of power, Adorno's future as a German academic grew increasingly precarious. Horkheimer's Institute was among the first intellectual groups to flee Germany, going first to Geneva and then New York, where it established a loose connection with Columbia University. Branches in Paris, where the *Zeitschrift* continued to be published until the war, and London, meant that its ties to Europe were not entirely severed. A number of collaborators, including Adorno, remained in Europe as long as they could. Adorno, in fact, seems to have naively hoped that the Nazis were a passing phenomenon and he might still salvage his career. After an abortive effort to transfer his *venia legendi* to Vienna, he settled for temporary exile in England, where he was reduced to the status of an 'advanced student' at

Merton College, Oxford. He still made frequent trips back to Germany, however, especially to Berlin to visit Gretel Karplus, whom he was to marry in 1937.

Although Adorno's rudimentary English meant he had little contact with the Oxford philosophical community, whose intellectual concerns he scarcely shared, he used the time in England to return to his earlier interest in Husserl and produce the first draft of a book published only in 1956 called, to translate it literally, *Metacritique of Epistemology*.[15] As in his Kierkegaard study, Adorno sought to discover the social underpinnings of the seemingly inexplicable fissures and antinomies in his subject's work, an intention captured in the concept of a 'metacritique' that surpassed a purely epistemological reflection. Treating Husserl's phenomenology as the most advanced instance of the decay of bourgeois idealism, he interpreted Husserl's insistence on bracketing historical considerations in the search for a universal, transcendental truth as a function of the specific historical crisis of the European middle class. Emphasizing in particular Husserl's desire for ultimate philosophical foundations, transcendental first principles, Adorno linked it with the yearning of Husserl's erstwhile student Heidegger for a restoration of man's opening to Being. He damned both for factoring out social reality and covertly giving priority to the subject, despite their intentions. Husserl, however, was superior to Heidegger, in his refusal to turn his epistemological quest into a full-fledged ontology. Husserl's important *Crisis of the European Sciences and Transcendental Philosophy,* which appeared when Adorno was in England, contained a critique of positivism and scientism that many commentators have seen as comparable to that of the Frankfurt School, but Adorno chose not to discuss anything Husserl wrote after 1931. It was not, in fact, until much later that a second-generation Critical Theorist, Jürgen Habermas, would recover aspects of the phenomenological tradition to rescue its critical potential, especially in Husserl's concept of a

Lebenswelt (life world) prior to scientific reflection.[16] Although Adorno may have admired Husserl for his un-flinching exposure of the aporias of late bourgeois thought, he denied that his still idealist philosophy pointed to any possible solutions.

Horkheimer and Marcuse were also increasingly dis-tancing themselves from their early interest in phenomenology, which had been particularly powerful in the latter's case when he was a student of Heidegger's in the last years of Weimar. Adorno's links with his Institute friends, in fact, remained very strong during his Oxford years. He contributed two articles to the *Zeitschrift*, 'On Jazz', written in 1936, and 'On the Fetish Character of Music and the Regression of Hearing', which appeared two years later.[17] Although Adorno had nothing directly to do with the Institute's major research project of those years, published as *Studies on Authority and Family* in 1936, one of the main concepts developed in it by the psychologist Erich Fromm, that of the sado-masochistic character, found its way into his work.

Adorno was also involved in the mid-1930s in the Insti-tute's complicated relationship with Benjamin, who re-mained in Paris where he was working on his massive study of that city in the nineteenth century, his never completed *Passagenwerk*.[18] In a series of now celebrated letters, the two friends discussed the merits of Benjamin's initial formulations of his position, raising many essential questions about Marxist aesthetics along the way.[19] Adorno, who was troubled by Benjamin's growing attrac-tion to the more militant politics and less sophisticated theory of Brecht, wrote 'On the Fetish Character' as an indirect reply to his friend's earlier contribution to the *Zeitschrift*, 'On the Work of Art in the Era of Mechanical Reproduction'.[20]

Adorno, however, was at one with Benjamin in his reluctance to follow Horkheimer and the Institute to New York. 'On Jazz' was written under the pseudonym Hektor Rottweiler, which perhaps expressed Adorno's still

33

flickering hope to find a position back in Germany. In fact, his decision during those years to drop his patronymic Wiesengrund in favour of his mother's name was interpreted by another refugee, Hannah Arendt, as evidence of an almost collaborationist mentality.[21] Although this conjecture is highly implausible, especially because the Institute's assistant director, Friedrich Pollock, has claimed that it was on *his* initiative that the name change took place,[22] it is true that Adorno was slow to sever his ties with Europe. As his article on jazz clearly demonstrated, he had no love for American culture, a prejudice that he never really overcame.

A brief visit to New York in June 1937 on Horkheimer's invitation did, however, help him allay his fears about continuing in the United States the type of intellectual work he had done in Europe. When Horkheimer telegraphed him later that year about a job opening, Adorno hesitated only briefly before accepting. When he arrived in February 1938, he discovered that the position, which was as part-time director of the music division of Princeton University's Radio Research Project led by Paul Lazarsfeld, was not precisely what he had expected.[23] Lazarsfeld, himself a recent émigré from Austria, was a master of empirical social science techniques, which he urged Adorno to use to test his speculations about music and mass culture. The incompatibilities between Lazarsfeld's ostensibly apolitical 'administrative research' and Adorno's critical alternative were, however, too profound to permit the collaboration to succeed. Adorno found it impossible to test his essentially Hegelian Marxist insights about reification, commodity fetishism and false consciousness through questionnaires addressed to their victims. Although he gained for the first time a grudging ability to use empirical methods, Adorno's role on the project was terminated in 1940, when its sponsor, the Rockefeller Foundation, withdrew its support from the musical section. He managed, however, to salvage four articles on radio music from the wreckage.[24]

Adorno's links with Horkheimer's Institute proved to be much more strongly forged. In the last two volumes of the *Zeitschrift*, which appeared from late 1939 to 1941 under the name *Studies in Philosophy and Social Science*, he contributed essays on Wagner, Kierkegaard, Spengler and Veblen.[25] His new work demonstrated his increasing closeness to Horkheimer, the Wagner study, for example, being clearly indebted to Horkheimer's 1936 essay on 'Egoism and the Freedom Movement',[26] which discussed proto-fascist elements in early bourgeois culture. Working closely with Horkheimer for the first time, Adorno began in subtle ways to qualify some of the positions he had inherited from Benjamin. Not only did he dissent from Benjamin's more optimistic politics, with their over-estimation of the progressive implications of modern technology for mass culture, he also began to reread Hegel, against whom Benjamin had always harboured considerable animosity. The result was a certain affirmation of the active, reflective subject whose threatened liquidation Benjamin with his more objectivist and Surrealist inclinations had refused to mourn. Although Adorno did not embrace Lukács's more genuinely Hegelian notion of a collective meta-subject, which was assumed to be the proletariat, he nonetheless insisted on the importance of preserving subjectivity, at least in its individual form, in a way that Benjamin did not.

Paradoxically, it was when Benjamin, deeply shocked by the Hitler-Stalin pact, retreated from his militancy of the mid-1930s and began again to introduce explicitly theological motifs into his work that Adorno's position came once more to converge with his. Shortly before he committed suicide on the French-Spanish border in September 1940, while en route to America and a closer affiliation with the Institute, Benjamin wrote a series of eighteen 'Historical-Philosophical Theses'. In this remarkable work, which the Institute printed in a limited-edition memorial collection dedicated to Benjamin in 1942,[27] he challenged the faith in historical progress that

35

had been so fundamental a part of the Marxist tradition. Redemption from oppression, Benjamin suggested, could come only by exploding the continuum of history through the messianic interruption of what he called '*Jetztzeit*', or 'Now-time', the mystical *nunc stans* that was the opposite of empty chronological time. Adorno, for all his continued sympathy for Hegelian dialectics and distrust of Benjamin's unremitting anti-individualism, was nonetheless in agreement with his critique of progressive historicism. He also found himself at one with his friend's emphasis on the link between the belief in historical progress and the domination of nature, against which utopian socialists such as Fourier had protested more than Marx. And he found himself completely in accord with Benjamin's dark observation that 'there is no document of civilization which is not at the same time a document of barbarism'.[28]

In the decade following Benjamin's suicide, which was a deep personal blow to Adorno, much of his work focused on the implications of these ideas, which were also embodied in the unfinished *Passagenwerk* manuscript that came into his hands at this time. In 1941, he moved to southern California to join Horkheimer and Pollock, who had moved there because of the former's uncertain health. From 1941 to 1944, Adorno and Horkheimer collaborated closely on a major statement of their now common position, which drew significantly on Benjamin's final ruminations. *Dialectic of Enlightenment*, first published in 1947 but not widely read until the 1960s, indicated to many the Frankfurt School's growing disenchantment with Marxism, even in its heterodox forms, and its concomitant embrace of what Benjamin, many years earlier in his more militant period, had attacked as 'left melancholia'.[29] The economic basis for their shift had been given by Pollock in several essays he contributed to the *Zeitschrift* on 'state capitalism'.[30] Although not contending that capitalism had resolved all of its contradictions, he intimated that state intervention in the economy had allowed it to contain and displace them indefinitely. The choice, Pollock suggested, was between democratic and authoritarian versions of state capitalism, rather than between capitalism *per se* and socialism.

In *Dialectic of Enlightenment,* Horkheimer and Adorno reached even gloomier conclusions about the ways in which Western society had undermined its emancipatory potential. In terms that harked back as much to Nietzsche and Weber as Marx, they explored the unexpectedly pernicious effect of rationality – understood in its instrumental, subjective sense – in producing the present crisis. The more substantive and synthetic reason, which German Idealism had called *Vernunft* in opposition to the merely analytical *Verstand* (intellect or understanding), had been, to borrow the title of a book by Horkheimer written during the same years, eclipsed.[31] However much rationality had sought to free man from mythic thinking, he remained caught in its nexus. Enlightenment had inadvertently produced its opposite for two basic reasons. First, instrumental reason was closely related to the exchange principle in which everything was reduced to an abstract equivalent of everything else in the service of universal exchange. Or, to put it in terms that Adorno would frequently employ, the qualitatively different and non-identical was forced into the mould of quantitative identity. One of its most prominent victims was the unique individual, which had come into its own during the heroic period of bourgeois ascendancy. Horkheimer and Adorno treated its passing in a highly nuanced way, both mourning its loss and recognizing its limitations. But they had little use for the various forms of collective pseudo-subjectivity that had replaced it.

The second source of instrumental reason's inadvertently destructive effect was its link with the domination of nature. Insofar as the natural world was reduced to a field of fungible entities, whose qualitative differences were lost in the name of scientific control, subjective domination of objects paved the way for the comparable

37

domination of subjects through reification. Domination of the external natural world led to control of man's internal nature and ultimately of the social world as well. Fascism, Horkheimer and Adorno argued, could in fact be partly understood as the return of man's repressed mythic past and the revenge of dominated nature, which employed many of the tools developed by instrumental reason in the service of that domination. 'Progress' thus turned out to spawn its antithesis, a barbarism all the more brutal because of its use of modern techniques of control. Science, rather than being an unequivocal force for human betterment, proved to contain the seeds of a new form of dehumanization. One of its preconditions was the obliterated memory of a state in which nature was not yet dominated by instrumental reason. In fact, 'all reification', Horkheimer and Adorno insisted in one of their most widely quoted remarks, 'is a forgetting'.[32]

In the allegedly democratic countries of the capitalist world, the dialectic of enlightenment produced that forgetting in more subtle ways than in their authoritarian rivals, but the results were no less regrettable. Through what Horkheimer and Adorno called the 'culture industry', mass consciousness was manipulated and distorted to the point where critical thinking was threatened with extermination. With a passion that had previously been expressed only by right-wing critics of mass culture, they denounced the insidious ways in which popular entertainment demeaned and cheated its consumers. Standardization and pseudo-individualization belied the claims of mass culture to cater to individual tastes. Virtually all levels of culture, in fact, were permeated by the process of commodification that Marx had identified in the nineteenth century. In what Adorno called the 'administered world', the prototype for what Marcuse was later to make famous as 'one-dimensional society', the permeation of ideology had gone so far that all resistance was virtually eliminated.

The 'ticket mentality' that characterized the victims of

the culture industry could be compared, so Horkheimer
and Adorno claimed, to the anti-Semitic mentality that
had fed fascism. Anti-Semitism, in fact, was now for the
first time a central concern of the Institute, which had
generally endorsed the standard Marxist explanations of
its importance through the 1930s.[33] During the war, however, they came to acknowledge its deeper and more
varied roots, without, to be sure, denying its links with the
economic role of the Jews under capitalism. They insisted
that the 'anti-Semitic question', a locution they preferred
to the more ambiguous 'Jewish question', could only be
fully understood by situating it in the larger context of the
dialectic of enlightenment. The Jews, Horkheimer and
Adorno argued, were prime targets of the totalitarian
identity principle of instrumental rationality because they
were the most resolute repository of otherness and difference in the Western world.

'Elements of Anti-Semitism', the theoretical section of
Dialectic of Enlightenment written with the help of Leo
Lowenthal, was complemented in indirect ways by the
Institute's work on an empirical project designed to investigate the same issues. In 1944, the American Jewish
Committee hired Horkheimer as the director of its newly
created Department of Scientific Research. Under his
guidance, the department launched a multi-volume series
of *Studies in Prejudice,* whose most important
achievement was the massive analysis of *The Authoritarian Personality.*[34] Adorno was the Institute's main collaborator on the project, which was conducted jointly with
the Berkeley Public Opinion Study Group led by R.
Nevitt Sanford, Daniel Levinson and Else Frenkel-
Brunswik. Although he left most of the actual empirical
testing to his co-workers, Adorno had overcome much of
his hostility to the type of research that he had been asked
to do by Lazarsfeld when he first came to America. The
project, however, went beyond mere data-gathering by
using psychoanalytic categories to interpret the results.
Here the earlier contribution of Erich Fromm to the Insti-

tute's *Studies on Authority and Family* was, at least in part, a model, even though his former colleagues had broken with Fromm in the interim.

Constructing a series of indicators that culminated in the celebrated 'F-Scale' (F standing for Fascism), Adorno and his collaborators attempted to create a research tool to uncover covert inclinations towards authoritarianism. The carefully worked-out questionnaires were complemented by in-depth interviews with selected individuals, whose results Adorno interpreted using the methods he had honed on other cultural and social phenomena. Essential to his analysis was the assumption that a constellation of related traits, such as conventionalism, submissiveness to authority, destructiveness and cynicism, were symptomatic of an anti-democratic character structure. The study immediately became an object of enormous controversy, which in part centred on its alleged over-emphasis of the subjective and psychological causes of authoritarianism. The Institute's Marxist roots were indeed less apparent in this project than in its earlier work, but a close reading of the sections written by Adorno would have revealed that it had not really abandoned its stress on objective as well as subjective factors. The work also had the ironic effect of identifying Adorno in the minds of most Americans with the type of social scientific research that was peripheral at best to his main interests.

These interests were more directly expressed in three other works he completed during his years in California. *Philosophy of Modern Music, Composing for the Films* (written jointly with Hanns Eisler), and *Minima Moralia*.[35] In 1941, Adorno had written a lengthy essay on 'Schoenberg and Progress', which both expanded on his earlier admiration for the composer and subtly introduced a new note of caution about the implications of his most recent work. The hypostatization of the twelve-tone row into a new compositional system by some of Schoenberg's disciples, Adorno now contended, threatened to undo the liberating effects of his earlier atonality. In 1948, Adorno wrote a companion piece on the other great twentieth-century composer, who had already been contrasted with Schoenberg as his polar opposite by Arthur Lourié, Igor Stravinsky. Together with an introductory essay, the two pieces were published in 1948 as *Philosophy of Modern Music*, which Adorno called an 'extended appendix' to *Dialectic of Enlightenment*.

However ambivalent Adorno may have been about the implications of Schoenberg's legacy, he was unequivocally hostile to that of Stravinsky. The latter, Adorno claimed, had revelled in the sacrifice of subjectivity whose pain Schoenberg had registered and resisted. The regressive sado-masochism of Stravinsky's restoration of archaic, neo-classical form, expressed a latent identification with the authoritarianism of late bourgeois society that surpassed even that of Wagner. For all his modernist intentions, Stravinsky was thus objectively in accord with *volkisch* and even neo-fascist tendencies.

Not surprisingly, admirers of Stravinksy like Robert Craft were highly critical of Adorno's analysis.[36] No less so was Schoenberg, who first learned about it indirectly when Thomas Mann, a fellow exile in California, appropriated Adorno's manuscript in the writing of his novel *Doctor Faustus*, published in 1947.[37] Schoenberg, sensing the critical note in his former disciple's account, was also outraged because Mann had failed to acknowledge him as the original source of the musical ideas he attributed to the novel's main character, Adrian Leverkühn. Schoenberg angrily denounced Adorno as an 'informer' who had somehow leaked sensitive musical material to Mann. The novelist, who had shown his gratitude to Adorno by using his patronymic Wiesengrund as the verbal illustration of a musical theme, tried to appease Schoenberg in subsequent editions of the work by acknowledging the music's ultimate provenance.

Adorno was far more circumspect in his dealings with another fellow refugee, the Marxist composer Hanns

41

128298

Adorno

Eisler, with whom he had been friends since they were introduced by Berg in 1925. Eisler, originally a follower of Schoenberg's 'new music', had turned against it as too elitist, in favour of more accessible 'proletarian choruses' with lyrics by Brecht. In his first essay in the *Zeitschrift*, Adorno had cautioned against this agitationally intended, affirmative type of art, which he linked with the reactionary 'community music' of composers like Hindemith. Eisler had been piqued enough to suggest several years later to Brecht that the Institute could serve as the model for his 'Tui' novel about hypocritical radical intellectuals who were really supported by the forces they purported to despise.

In their common exile, however, Adorno and Eisler buried their differences enough to collaborate in 1944 on a study of film music, innocently sponsored by the generous benefactor of so many refugee projects, the Rockefeller Foundation. The book combined a typically Adornoesque critique of standardized musical stereotypes with a more Brechtian insistence on the possibility of undermining them through exposing their mechanisms. Adorno seems, however, to have felt uncomfortable with this practically oriented dimension of the book. When *Composing for the Films* was published in 1947, at a time when Eisler's brother Gerhard was under attack for his Communist affiliations, the anxious Adorno left his name off the title page. A year later, his co-author emigrated to East Germany, where he brought out a revised edition without any credit to Adorno. Only when the book appeared in West Germany in 1969 was Adorno's role in its creation fully acknowledged.

The often painful relations between émigrés exemplified by these episodes were in part responsible for Adorno's bitter ruminations on the exile experience in the series of 153 aphorisms he published in 1951 as *Minima Moralia: Reflections from Damaged Life*. This most Nietzschean of Adorno's work expressed in subjective and often ironic form the dilemmas of his permanent exile.

42

Although Adorno had joined his Institute colleagues in acquiring American citizenship, he never genuinely felt comfortable in his adopted surroundings. Recognizing the temptation of refugees to indulge their self-pity, and never forgetting the fate of friends like Benjamin who failed to emigrate, he nonetheless mourned the fact that 'every intellectual in emigration is, without exception, mutilated, and does well to acknowledge it to himself, if he wishes to avoid being cruelly apprised of it behind the tightly closed doors of his self-esteem'.[38]

Minima Moralia, which many commentators praised as Adorno's finest stylistic achievement, also contained brilliantly formulated encapsulations of theoretical arguments which he developed at greater length elsewhere. None perhaps was as celebrated as his claim that, contra Hegel, 'the whole is the false,'[39] which demonstrated his movement away from the Hegelian Marxism of Lukács and the early Horkheimer. The micrological emphasis of Kracauer and Benjamin, with their suspicion of any holistic pretensions, was now clearly uppermost in Adorno's mind. It was also in *Minima Moralia* that Adorno registered his fear that the method of immanent ideology critique, the comparison of ideologies with their alleged realization which he had used so frequently in his earlier work, was itself losing the capacity to provide a truly critical leverage on the world. 'Irony's medium,' he wrote, 'the difference between ideology and reality, has disappeared. The former resigns itself to confirmation of reality by its mere duplication. . . . There is not a crevice in the cliff of the established order into which the ironist might hook a fingernail.'[40]

If there were any relief from the bitter implications of these observations, it came only indirectly in his admission that essential to any valid cognition is 'an element of exaggeration, of over-shooting the object, of self-detachment from the weight of the factual'.[41] Thus, despite the apparently seamless pessimism of such works as *Dialectic of Enlightenment* and *Minima Moralia,*

43

Adorno

Adorno never completely abandoned his hope that radical change was still possible. However often he may have called the world a delusional system (*Verblendungs- zusammenhang*), he refused to make it absolutely impervious to negation. As he put it in a piece written in 1951 on 'Freudian Theory and the Pattern of Fascist Propaganda', the increase in ideologically and psychologically controlled domination 'may well terminate in sudden awareness of the untruth of the spell, and eventually in its collapse'.[42]

It was at least in part because of this refusal to resign himself entirely that Adorno, along with Horkheimer and Pollock, decided to return to Germany and rebuild the Institute in 1949. Marcuse, Lowenthal, and other former Institute figures like Erich Fromm, Karl August Wittfogel, Franz Neumann and Otto Kirchheimer all chose to remain in America, where they ultimately achieved considerable recognition. Of all their colleagues, only one, the economist Henryk Grossmann, went to the Russian zone of their divided homeland, which illustrates the hostility they continued to have to Soviet versions of Marxism. In later years, when the Frankfurt School became a powerful stimulus to libertarian socialist movements in Europe, Communist spokesmen would return their animosity in kind.[43]

The stormy future of the revived Institute of Social Research would have been difficult to prophesy in 1949. The city of Frankfurt, anxious to lure back survivors of Weimar culture, welcomed Horkheimer and his colleagues with considerable enthusiasm. Supported in part by funds from the American High Commissioner John J. McCloy, the Institute officially reopened its doors in 1951 in a building not far from the bombed-out ruins of its predecessor. In the same year, Horkheimer was elected rector of the University; when his two-year tenure ended, he was awarded one of the city's highest honours, its Goethe Medal, later given to Adorno and Lowenthal as well.

44

Adorno, it will be recalled, had always been anxious to return to Germany, in large measure because of his belief that his native tongue was the most appropriate medium in which to express dialectical thought. Although he spent a year back in Los Angeles in 1952, working for the Hacker Foundation on social psychological analyses of popular culture,[44] Adorno's exile, at least in literal terms, was now at an end. But in a deeper cultural and psychological sense, his inability to feel truly at home anywhere in the 'administered world' meant that even back in the city of his youth he remained at odds with his environment.

Ironically, the initial expression of this tension appeared as a result of his efforts and those of his collaborators to introduce to Germany the very empirical techniques that Adorno had so vigorously resisted during his unhappy partnership with Lazarsfeld in the late 1930s.[45] Embedded, to be sure, in a theoretical framework, such techniques could have a progressive effect in a country where simple facts had been systematically distorted and ignored for so many years. To combat the general West German amnesia about what soon became known as its 'unmastered past', it was necessary to educate Germans about the unpalatable realities of the Nazi era, as well as their extension into the present. To this end, the Institute established a specifically empirical branch in 1956 under the direction of Rudolf Gunzert. In so doing, the Institute hoped to disseminate the methods it had developed in the *Studies in Prejudice* series, to help the Germans confront the deeper sources of their attraction to fascism.

Adorno and his colleagues also sought to persuade their new German audience that the insights of psychoanalysis should be marshalled in this cause.[46] In America Freud had been perverted into an anti-political defender of the status quo, who allegedly preached adjustment to an external reality that could not be changed. Even Fromm's earlier attempt to synthesize him with Marx, so his former

45

colleagues now believed,[47] had inadvertently produced the same effect. But in Germany, where psychoanalysis had been suppressed as a degenerate 'Jewish science', its implications were still explosive. Not only would it help reveal the tangled roots of the Germans' attraction to Hitler, it would also allow contemporary Germans to deal with what the Frankfurt psychoanalysts and Institute friends Alexander and Margarete Mitscherlich called their 'inability to mourn'.[48] In 1956, the Institute took the occasion of Freud's hundredth birthday to sponsor a conference, which attracted distinguished analysts like Erik Erikson and Franz Alexander. As one of the attentive listeners, Jürgen Habermas, later recalled, '"Freud in the Present" was the first opportunity for young German academics to learn about the simple fact that Sigmund Freud was the founding father of a living scientific and intellectual tradition.'[49]

The more radical, even utopian implications of that tradition, which one participant in the conference, Herbert Marcuse, had just emphasized in his book *Eros and Civilization,* were not, however, equally stressed by Horkheimer and Adorno. In fact, the returning members of the Institute were generally reticent about publicizing the Marxist aspects of their previous work. When they launched a new series of *Frankfurt Contributions to Sociology,* they deliberately chose not to include a translation of such Institute-sponsored projects as Franz Neumann's *Behemoth,*[50] whose analysis of Nazism largely in terms of monopoly capitalism seemed too simplistic (or too provocative in the Cold War atmosphere of the 1950s). Equally symptomatic, the Institute's collectively written volume in the series, *Aspects of Sociology,*[51] included a chapter on the masses, but not one on classes. As early as 1951, members of the Institute who remained in America had noted a subtle change in its orientation. When Lowenthal complained that the empirical research techniques Horkheimer was now so vigorously supporting were at odds with Critical Theory, the Institute director defensively replied, 'We stand here for the good things: for individual independence, the idea of the Enlightenment, science freed from blinders. When you and other friends see the type of empirical social science we are conducting here as in many ways conventional, I am convinced that you would be of another opinion could you see the thing with your own eyes.'[52]

For the co-author of *Dialectic of Enlightenment* to assert his support for 'the idea of the Enlightenment' suggests how far the Institute had gone in moderating its earlier hostility to bourgeois values, at least in the context of rebuilding a democratic Germany. Symbolic of Horkheimer's caution was his decision to keep the more politically explosive volumes of the *Zeitschrift*, according to Habermas, 'in a crate in the Institute's cellar, nailed shut, and out of our grasp'.[53] Horkheimer, in fact, steadfastly refused to allow the republication of his essays from those years until 1968, when he agreed to do so only after affixing a preface which warned that 'thoughtless and dogmatic application of Critical Theory to practice in changed historical circumstances can only accelerate the very process which the theory aimed at denouncing'.[54] And even then, he still balked at the republication of his controversial essay of 1939 on 'The Jews and Europe', which contained the widely cited remark, 'He who does not wish to speak of capitalism should also be silent about fascism.'[55]

By this time, however, most of the Institute's more explicitly Marxist work of the 1930s and still radical writings of the 1940s had appeared in pirated editions brought out by German New Leftists. These illegal, but widely circulated texts did much to consolidate the image of 'the Frankfurt School' (a term that only gained currency in the 1960s) as an intransigent critic of both orthodox Marxism and liberal democracy. The utopian impulses of Critical Theory, which Marcuse in particular still fervently defended, were revived to serve as the stimulus for many of the demands of Germany's libertarian left.

47

Adorno's own contribution to this process was not merely confined to the reluctant reproduction of earlier, more militant writings. Unlike Horkheimer, he had no compunctions about publishing potentially explosive works written during his exile.[56] Although their relationship was never closer, Adorno did not adopt his friend's somewhat apologetic embrace of religion. Nor did he relax his even-handed hostility towards both existing socialist and capitalist systems in the work he wrote after his return to Frankfurt. In 1952, for example, the complete text of *In Search of Wagner* was published, still bearing the influence of Horkheimer's 1936 essay on 'Egoism and the Freedom Movement'.[57] No less prominent in Adorno's analysis were Marx's concept of commodity fetishism and Lukács's notion of reification, which he used to explain the phantasmagoric aspects of Wagner's music.

In 1955, a collection of essays entitled *Prisms: Cultural Criticism and Society* appeared, containing treatments of a wide variety of subjects including Mannheim, Spengler, Veblen, Kafka, George, Hofmannsthal, Schoenberg, Huxley, Bach and jazz.[58] In the programmatic essay that began the collection, 'Cultural Criticism and Society', Adorno continued the Institute's attack on what Horkheimer and Marcuse had called 'affirmative culture' in the 1930s.[59] Vigorously rejecting the fetish of high culture as a realm above material concerns, he insisted in terms showing his lingering indebtedness to Hegelian Marxism that 'what distinguishes dialectical from cultural criticism is that it heightens cultural criticism until the notion of culture is itself negated, fulfilled and surmounted in one'.[60] Reflecting on the implications of the Holocaust, Adorno went even further than his Institute colleagues had gone in the interwar era in denouncing the fraudulence of culture. Echoing Benjamin's remark in the 'Historical-Philosophical Theses', he concluded that cultural criticism finds itself faced with the final stage of the dialectic of culture and barbarism. To write poetry after Auschwitz is barbaric. And this corrodes even the knowledge of why it has become impossible to write poetry today. Absolute reification, which presupposed intellectual progress as one of its elements, is now preparing to absorb the mind entirely.[61]

Prisms also contained Adorno's first major consideration of Benjamin, a collection of whose writings he, along with his wife Gretel, brought out in the same year.[62] Although the essay was not without its critical barbs, directed largely at Benjamin's Surrealist sympathies and his exaggerated hostility towards individual subjectivity, it helped establish his importance as twentieth-century Germany's most original cultural critic. In later years, Adorno would be embroiled in a bitter controversy over his alleged manipulation of Benjamin's legacy in a non-Marxist direction, but even his detractors could not deny his essential role, along with that of Gershom Scholem, in rescuing Benjamin from undeserved oblivion.

Nor could they dispute Adorno's Promethean energies in demonstrating the power and range of his own radical critique of culture, which in many ways drew on Benjamin's legacy. Beginning in 1956 with *Dissonances: Music in the Administered World* and 1958 with the first of four volumes of *Notes on Literature*,[63] Adorno regularly published an astounding number of monographs and essay collections on musical and literary themes. Combining new work with older manuscripts that had been unfinished or published in inaccessible places, Adorno brought out in rapid succession *Tone Configurations* (1959), *Mahler: a Musical Physiognomy* (1960), *Notes on Literature II* (1961), *Introduction to the Sociology of Music* (1962), *Interventions: Nine Critical Models* (1963), *The Loyal Musical Coach: Pedagogical Writings on Musical Praxis* (1963), *Quasi una Fantasia: Musical Writings II* (1963), *Musical Moments: Newly Published Essays from 1928 to*

1962 (1964), *Notes on Literature III* (1965), *Without Model: Parva Aesthetica* (1967), *Berg: the Master of the Smallest Transitions* (1968), *Impromptus: Second Series of Newly Published Musical Essays* (1968), *Keywords: Critical Models II* (1969), and *Nerve Points of the New Music* (1969).[64] There were also enough materials still left in manuscript form when he died in 1969 to fill several more volumes in the collected works launched with *Aesthetic Theory* in 1970.

At the same time as Adorno was flooding Germany with his writings on cultural issues, he actively continued his contribution to the restoration of postwar German sociology. Here too the still radical dimension of his work had not lost its potency. 'Society', he insisted, 'remains class society today just as in the period when the concept originated.'[65] In fact, by the late 1950s, Adorno began to have qualms about the Institute's earlier emphasis on disseminating American social science techniques in Germany. The task had been successfully accomplished, perhaps too successfully, and empiricism threatened to replace rather than supplement theory. In 1957, Adorno published an essay entitled 'Sociology and Empirical Research',[66] which challenged the assumption that theoretical and empirical arguments could be placed on a smooth continuum. Expanding on a similar contention he had made two years earlier in a discussion of the complicated relationship between sociology and psychology,[67] he argued that the fissures and contradictions of the real world meant that no harmoniously conceived methodology could be adequate to its object. Thus, although empirical techniques could register certain limited truths about, say, the reactions of listeners to certain kinds of music, they could never reveal the underlying implications of the music itself. The whole may be the 'untrue', but it was still necessary to combine approaches to grasp its fractured dimensions. The combination, however, should not be that of a smoothly unified mediation of those approaches, but rather that of a force-field or constellation which registered the unresolved tensions behind the façade of harmony.[68]

In retrospect, Adorno's essay can be seen as the first sally in a vigorous controversy that was to split the German academic world in the 1960s. The 'positivist dispute', as it became known despite the unwillingness of any of its participants to call themselves positivists, was officially launched at the 1961 meeting of the German Sociological Association in Tübingen. The distinguished philosopher of science and long-time critic of dialectical thought, Karl Popper, spoke on 'The Logic of the Social Sciences' and Adorno, followed by Ralf Dahrendorf, replied. Along with Adorno's 1957 essay, subsequent interventions by Jürgen Habermas, Hans Albert and Harald Pilot, and new entries by Popper and Adorno, their remarks were collected in 1969 in a widely discussed book.[69] Both sides often seemed to speak past one another and mutual accusations of misinterpreting each other's position were frequent. But the dispute did clarify many of the issues separating Adorno's still dialectical version of Critical Theory from the Critical Rationalism of Popper and his followers. Along with a related debate over the implications of Max Weber's sociology that Frankfurt School members entered in 1964,[70] it helped confirm Adorno's status as a still fervent defender of a politically committed social theory. For whereas the Popperians contended that scientists in an 'open society' could engage in the rational pursuit of scientific truth (or more precisely, the falsification of scientific error), Adorno continued to insist that 'the idea of scientific truth cannot be split off from that of a true society'.[71]

At the same time as Adorno was engaging in this protracted polemic with Popper and his supporters over what he saw as their misguided universalization of the scientific method, he was fighting a no less heated war on another front with very different opponents, the phenomenologists and existentialists of Germany led by the formidable figure of Martin Heidegger. In 1956, Adorno finally published *Metacritique of Epistemology,* the extensive critique of Husserl he had begun at Oxford in the 1930s. It was followed eight years later by a polemic, far more savage in tone, aimed at *The Jargon of Authenticity.*[72] Extending the arguments he had made against Kierkegaard's defence of subjective inwardness to later existentialists such as Heidegger, Jaspers and Buber, he claimed that the post-war fascination with this discourse of authentic human relations had contributed to the mystification of the social conditions that prevented such authenticity from being achieved. There were, moreover, subterranean links between existentialist irrationalism and the cultural crisis that helped prepare the way for fascism. In particular, Heidegger's insistence on the ontological meaning of death betrayed a covert sympathy for a totalizing identity theory that denied difference even as it purported to defend it. 'Now, as earlier,' Adorno noted, 'that answer is valid which Horkheimer gave to an enthusiastic female devotee of Heidegger's. She said that Heidegger had finally, at least, once again placed man before death; Horkheimer replied that Ludendorff had taken care of that much better.'[73]

In the present, a greater threat came from the jargon's misleading claim to transcend the reality of reified subjectivity. Like the cult of lyric poetry, whose pretence to escape social penetration Adorno had challenged several years earlier,[74] it offered a pseudo-immediacy that ultimately served to perpetuate the social domination of the subject. Rather than negating the alienation of modern life, the jargon of authenticity was one of its more subtle manifestations.

That Adorno held out little hope for a reversal of this situation, which would lead to the achievement of a genuine subjectivity, was evident in the longer study of which *The Jargon of Authenticity* was originally to be a part. *Negative Dialectics,* published in 1966, brought together many of the themes of Adorno's philosophical work in as close to a sustained theoretical argument as he could allow himself. That such an argument could not, however, be presented in systematic, deductive form was still very much a guiding assumption of his method, which remained essentially essayistic in spirit. True to the programme announced in 'The Actuality of Philosophy', Adorno provided metacritical analyses of both idealist and Heideggerian ontologies in the name of an anti-metaphysical dialectic of non-identity, which resisted closure and reconciliation.

Negative Dialectics also contained dark meditations on the implication of Auschwitz for both metaphysics and Marxism. Adorno was unflinching in his confrontation of the melancholy fact that, as he put it in a widely quoted observation, 'philosophy, which once seemed obsolete, lives on because the moment to realize it was missed'.[75] It was in large measure because the return of that moment seemed little short of impossible for Adorno that many observers saw *Negative Dialectics* as a cul-de-sac, the terminal point of the Western Marxist tradition launched by Lukács and Korsch after the First World War. As one of his more hostile critics, Leszek Kolakowski, put it, 'There can be few works of philosophy that give such an overpowering impression of sterility as *Negative Dialectics*.'[76] If Adorno allowed any glimmer of hope, it was only in his references to art, which at least knew itself to be illusory. He wrote:

Art is semblance even at its highest peaks; but its semblance, the irresistible part of it, is given to it by what is not semblance. What art, notably the art decried as nihilistic, says in refraining from judgments is that everything is not just nothing. If it were, whatever is would be pale, colourless, indifferent. No light falls on men and things without reflecting transcendence. Indelible from the resistance to the fungible world of exchange is the resistance of the eye that does not want the colours of the world to fade. Semblance is a promise of nonsemblance.[77]

Adorno's last work, left unfinished at his death, was appropriately a treatise on *Aesthetic Theory*. Now often regarded as even more of a crowning achievement than *Negative Dialectics,* the work combined philosophical and sociological analyses to defend the critical power of modernist – or what he now called 'de-aestheticized' – art. An art that self-consciously debunked its illusory claim to wholeness and self-sufficiency was more capable of negating reality than one that kept up the pretence. Such an art, in fact, had certain advantages over a comparably negative philosophy, because it ran no risk of dominating the material world through its conceptual power. The mimetic dimension of art, its implicit tribute to the value of natural as opposed to entirely man-made beauty, prevented it from coercing nature in the same way that purely theoretical cognition tended to do. Indeed, in its very refusal to subordinate nature to thought, matter to spirit, de-aestheticized art provided a flickering utopian model of what mankind, despite everything, might become.

Adorno, even in his bleakest moments, thus refused to relinquish Critical Theory's desire for what Horkheimer called 'the entirely other' (*das ganz Andere*).[78] He continued to defend the importance of critical thinking as 'bottles thrown into the sea' for future addressees, whose identity was still unknown. Against his critics' contention that he had abandoned revolutionary practice – in which, to be sure, he had never directly engaged himself – Adorno replied:

> The uncompromisingly critical thinker, who neither subordinates his conscience nor permits himself to be terrorized into action, is in truth' the one who does not give up. . . . Open thinking points beyond itself. For its part, such thinking takes a position as a figuration of praxis which is more closely related to a praxis truly involved in change than is a position of mere obedience for the sake of praxis.[79]

For many activists in the German New Left and elsewhere, however, this 'strategy of hibernation',[80] as Habermas dubbed it, seemed woefully deficient. Adorno, hearing many of his more uncompromising criticisms of late capitalist society hurled back at him, plaintively lamented in a widely reported statement that only further infuriated his critics, 'When I made my theoretical model, I could not have guessed that people would want to realize it with Molotov cocktails.'[81] The weapons soon turned against Adorno himself were less obviously lethal, but had their effect nonetheless.

In April 1969, three members of a militant action group rushed on to the podium during one of his lectures, bared their breasts and 'attacked' him with flowers and erotic caresses. Adorno, unnerved and humiliated, left the lecture hall with the students mockingly proclaiming that 'as an institution, Adorno is dead'. The *Schadenfreude* of his enemies, both on the right and left, was considerable, foreshadowing the reaction of many critics of the Frankfurt School a few years later when the German terrorists of the 1970s were seen, much to the horror of the School's surviving members, as their responsibility.

Four months after the Frankfurt incident, the symbolic patricide became sadly real as Adorno, a month short of his sixty-sixth birthday, suffered a heart attack on vacation in Switzerland. Still at the height of his powers, he died without the concluding cadence, the harmonious reconciliation, so insistently negated by his philosophy. In this sense, perhaps Adorno's end fittingly suited a life devoted to resisting the death-like power of the false totality.

2. Atonal Philosophy

'Die Systeme sind für die kleinen Leute. Die grossen haben die Intuition: sie setzten auf die Nummern, die ihnen einfallen. . . . Ihren Intuitionen sind zuverlässiger als die mühsamen Kalkulationen der Armen, die immer daran scheitern, dass man sie nicht gründlich durchprobieren kann.'[1]
HEINRICH REGIUS

'Karl Marx was a German philosopher.'[2] So Leszek Kolakowski begins his magisterial account of the *Main Currents of Marxism*. The same can certainly be said of Theodor Adorno, but behind the identity there lurks a substantial difference. For the Germany of Adorno's day was a far cry from that of Marx's and the philosophy appropriate to each age was radically dissimilar. Briefly stated, whereas Marx lived at a time when a disunited, 'backward' Germany sought to realize the promises of greatness contained in the ambitious systems of its idealist metaphysicians, Adorno was alive when a much chastened philosophy had to make sense as best it could of the monstrous failure of that attempt. No less sobering were the philosophical implications of an equally troubling catastrophe: the miscarrying of Marx's own expectation that the true realization of German philosophy would occur not with the mere achievement of national greatness, but rather with the triumph of a genuinely universal class through a proletarian revolution. Thus, while Marx had written at a moment when philosophy was energetically and aggressively descending into the material world, confident of the imminent unity of theory and

56

practice, Adorno's philosophizing was carried out amidst the ruins of what seemed a very unfortunate fall.

Rather, however, than seek to remove philosophy once again from the baser realm of historical contingency, Adorno stubbornly insisted that its fatal entanglement with the world was an irreversible development that must be squarely, if painfully, faced. His task then was to find a way to preserve the critical power of a philosophy that was immanent in a fallen world, a philosophy that was thoroughly historical yet could brush against the grain of what he saw as our century's bleak and tragic history. Much of the dynamism of his thought, as well as many of its unresolved tensions, resulted from the difficulty of this endeavour.

Although Adorno emphasized the dialectical relationship between history and philosophy, his own thought remained surprisingly constant for virtually all of his mature life. There is thus no significant 'young-old' problem for Adorno scholarship, as there is for that of Marx, Hegel, Lukács and Benjamin, to mention four figures who have lent themselves to this kind of periodization. Although a more detailed reconstruction of his development than can be offered here would pay some attention to the shifts in nuance and emphasis that did inevitably occur, a compact one such as this can assume a basic unity of outlook throughout his corpus without doing too much violence to the truth. To gain an avenue of entry into his philosophy, it is thus possible to pick a shorter work and examine it closely rather than attempt to summarize and paraphrase his *oeuvre* as a whole. Indeed, insofar as Adorno frequently stressed the essayistic quality of his work,[3] because of its experimental and open form, it is especially appropriate to focus on a seemingly 'minor' piece in order to capture his larger argument.

A particularly useful text for this purpose is the densely argued essay entitled 'Subject-Object', which was published in the collection entitled *Keywords* in the year of Adorno's death and is now available in English in *The*

Essential Frankfurt School Reader.[4] Although focused on a specific issue in the theory of knowledge, the essay contains a distillation of many of the central problems and arguments of Adorno's philosophy, which in fact was often cast, to borrow the original title of his critique of Husserl, as a 'metacritique of epistemology'. As we noted earlier, metacritique meant going beyond the realm of philosophy *per se* into its social and historical underpinnings, without, however, reducing it to them in the manner of a vulgar sociology of knowledge. 'Subject-Object' is in this regard an exemplary piece. It is no less typical of Adorno's demanding style, with its paratactic and untotalized construction. By following the apparently shapeless quality of the argument rather than forcing on it a more pleasingly coherent form, we will remain truer to Adorno's intention than we would by providing a smoothly articulated paraphrase. And by periodically going outside this specific text to others in Adorno's corpus, we will honour his injunction to situate examples of his argument in the larger context of his work as a whole.

The importance of the polarity in the essay's title for Adorno's entire work cannot be exaggerated. As Habermas has noted,[5] his was essentially a 'consciousness philosophy' concerned with the intricate problem, so central to both the idealist and critical Marxist traditions, of how subjects relate to objects in the present world and how they might relate to them in a possible future one. The scorn which Adorno and other members of the Frankfurt School often expressed for positivism in all its varieties resulted largely from what they saw as its inadequate treatment of this issue. To put the familiar argument in capsule form, positivism failed to recognize the active, constitutive power of subjectivity in creating the world (or more precisely, that part of it which we call history, culture and society), and thus was complicitous with a passive, contemplative politics which accepted the world as a finished reality, a 'second nature'.

Idealism, as Marx had recognized in his first Thesis on Feuerbach, had developed and preserved the active, practical side of subjectivity, which was neglected both by positivism and non-dialectical forms of materialism. But it had done so only on the abstract level of a transcendental or purely philosophical subjectivity. The task for Marx and later critical Marxists like Lukács was to identify the concrete historical embodiment of the active subjectivity posited by German Idealism. Whether or not they merely ascribed that role to the proletariat or broke more fundamentally with the idealist paradigm as a whole has been a well-gnawed bone of contention among Marxists and Marxologists ever since. Adorno appears to have believed that, to a dangerous extent, many Marxists did in fact replicate the idealist conceptualization of the subject-object problem in terms that violated their materialist intentions. His own role, as he understood it, was thus to call into question not only the passive, contemplative subject of the positivists, but also the overly active meta- or trans-individual constituting subject of the idealists and their Marxist offspring. As he put it in the Preface to *Negative Dialectics*, 'To use the strength of the subject to break through the fallacy of constitutive subjectivity – this was what the author felt to be his task ever since he came to trust his own mental impulses.'[6] A genuine materialism, as the Frankfurt School always contended, also had an ethical function; it must register and draw on the sufferings and needs of contingent human subjects rather than explain them away through an historiosophical theodicy.

'Subject-Object' begins precisely by examining the ambiguity of 'the subject'. Meaning both particular individual and consciousness in general, the term is inherently equivocal. For any reference to our individual ego entails a concept of the subject that has universal connotations, which thus takes it beyond the particular person. But any completely collective concept of the subject which suppresses individual difference fails to be adequate to its object in the real world, where those differences have not been entirely eradicated. It is thus impossible to avoid the term's polysemic indecisiveness (a conclusion that is strengthened still further if we introduce, as Adorno does not in this essay, the contradictory meanings of subject as active agent, the source of one's own destiny, and as passive object of domination, the plaything of an other to whose will one is 'subjected').[7]

Attempting to resolve these ambiguities by arbitrarily choosing one meaning and calling it more basic than the others, Adorno goes on to argue, would reproduce a philosophical aporia that has troubled thinkers ever since Kant:

> Defining means that something objective, no matter what it may be in itself, is subjectively captured by means of a fixed concept. Hence the resistance offered to defining by subject and object. To determine their meanings takes reflection on the very thing which definition cuts off for the sake of conceptual flexibility. Hence the advisability, at the outset, of taking up the words 'subject' and 'object' as the well-honed philosophical language hands them to us as a historical sediment. . . .[8]

The implications of this contention are twofold. First, any adequate theory of knowledge must recognize the impossibility of finding concepts perfectly congruous with the objects they attempt to describe; that consciousness of exaggeration we saw Adorno defending in *Minima Moralia* as a counterweight to the merely factual should thus accompany any valid epistemology. Second, rather than proceeding deductively from a series of carefully demarcated premises, philosophy must begin *in medias res* with the imperfect material presented by our contemporary historical situation. For as Benjamin once put it, 'Sundering truth from falsehood is the goal of the materialist method, not its point of departure. In other words, its point of departure is the object riddled with error, with *doxa* [conjecture].'[9] To move from error to truth requires a critique of concepts that pits their ambiguous implications against the social world to which they imperfectly refer; the result will not merely be that the concept is inadequate to the world, but also that the world as it presently is constituted is inadequate to certain meanings of the concept. It is the interaction of these complementary inadequacies that gives thought, so Adorno contended, its critical power to transcend the status quo.

The particular 'error' of contemporary epistemology that Adorno addresses in 'Subject-Object' is the radical separation of subject and object, which has been a fundamental assumption of Western thought at least since Descartes. By examining the implications of the separation outside of pure thought, however, one can see that it is 'both real and illusory. True, because in the cognitive realm it serves to express the real separation, the dichotomy of the human condition, a coercive development. False, because the resulting separation must not be hypostatized, not magically transformed into an invariant.'[10]

The apparent paradox becomes meaningful only if Adorno's idiosyncratic use of true and false, assumed but not spelled out in the essay, is grasped. Whereas truth in the first part of the statement refers to the state of the present world, falsehood in the second is based on his insistence, which we noted in our brief account of the 'positivist dispute' of the 1960s, that the idea of scientific truth was dependent on the future realization of a 'true' society. In other words, truth in what might be called a descriptive sense meant correspondence with things as they are, whereas in a normative sense it meant with things as they might be. It was this latter usage that underlay such remarks as 'the whole is the untrue', which registered Adorno's virtual abandonment of the Hegelian premise that within a dialectical description of the 'is' there is necessarily latent the normative 'ought'. Or more

61

precisely put, it was only in the traces, ruins and pre-figurations of some other reality that escaped the totalitarian power of the current whole that normative truth might be found. These ciphers of a possible redemption were not, however, securely grounded in an underlying ontological level, the 'not-yet-being' posited by Adorno's friend Ernst Bloch. Rather, they emerged only through the arduous process of interpretation that Adorno termed 'exact fantasy; fantasy which abides strictly within the material which the sciences present to it, and reaches beyond them only in the smallest aspects of their arrangement: aspects, granted, which fantasy itself must originally generate'.[11] Although such regenerative fantasizing courted the possibility of arbitrary wilfulness, as Adorno's critics often noted, it was the only way to preserve what he liked to call an 'emphatic concept of truth' at a time when it had fled from the 'false' whole of the present.

This flight, Adorno tells us in 'Subject-Object', had begun long before a fully 'administered world' had crystallized in our own century. In epistemological terms, it began for mankind with the separation of mind from the material world. 'Once radically parted from the object,' Adorno writes, 'the subject reduces it to its own measure; the subject swallows the object, forgetting how much it is an object itself.'[12] As he and Horkheimer had contended in *Dialectic of Enlightenment,* the domination of nature ensued once man's primal embeddedness in nature was transcended and then forgotten. A radical humanism carries with it the latent threat of species imperialism, which ultimately returns to haunt human relations themselves. Indeed, from the first, the domination of nature was intertwined with social hierarchy and control. In philosophical terms, this domination of the object by the subject is expressed both in positivism and idealism. In the former, a subjectivity stands coolly apart from its object in order to manipulate it; although seemingly passive, the positivist subject really has an instrumental relationship to the world, a world on which it unreflexively projects the scientifically ascertainable traits it claims merely to discover. In the latter, a more frankly constitutive subjectivity assumes that the world is the product of a consciousness that recognizes itself in its objective creations. Behind this assumption is a rage against the otherness of the natural world, which the allegedly sovereign mind tries to devour. In contrast to both positivism and idealism, a genuinely negative dialectics acknowledges what Adorno called 'the preponderance of the object'[13] irreducible to – although not entirely unmediated by – an active subjectivity.

But if Adorno was hostile to the absolute separation of subject and object, especially when it hid the covert domination of the object by the subject, his alternative model did not entail the perfect unity of the two concepts, or a return to an original embeddedness in nature. For all his own interest in the liberating power of remembrance, which he shared with other members of the Frankfurt School,[14] Adorno steadfastly refused to succumb to any nostalgia for a prehistorical era of plenitude and harmony. Whether it be the young Lukács's vision of epic wholeness in Homeric Greece, Heidegger's notion of a fulfilled Being now tragically forgotten, or even Benjamin's faith in a prelapsarian, Adamic oneness of name and thing, he remained deeply sceptical of any restoration of pre-reflective unity. With an almost proto-deconstructionist contempt for the metaphysics of perfect presence, 'Subject-Object' attacks all regressive yearnings:

The picture of a temporal or extratemporal original state of happy identity between subject and object is romantic, however – a wishful project at times, but today no more than a lie. The undifferentiated state before the subject's formation was the dread of the blind web of nature, of myth; it was in protest against it that the great religions had their truth content. Besides, to be undifferentiated is not to be one; even in Platonic

63

dialectics, unity requires diverse items of which it is the unity.[15]

In other words, for all the costs of leaving behind man's primal unity with nature, his departure was ultimately a progressive one. In making this point, 'Subject-Object' was also chastising those philosophies, including Hegelian Marxism, that sought a perfect oneness of man and world. For Adorno, any philosophy which lamented the lost origins of humanity's wholeness with the world or identified utopia with its future realization was not merely misguided, but potentially pernicious as well. For the obliteration of the distinction between subject and object would effectively mean the loss of the capacity for reflection that was no less its result than the alienation bemoaned by Marxist Humanists and others. The old idealist dream of a higher synthetic reason (*Vernunft*) as opposed to the analytic intellect or understanding (*Verstand*), a dream which certain Western Marxists had also shared, was thus not without its dangers if it became the model for a 'forced reconciliation' in the future. Even Lukács's theory of reification, which had been so influential in the formation of Critical Theory, was not free of this taint. In *Negative Dialectics* Adorno spelled out the reasons for his scepticism:

The category of reification, which was inspired by the wishful image of unbroken subjective immediacy, no longer merits the key position accorded to it, overzealously, by an apologetic thinking happy to absorb materialist thinking. . . . The total liquefaction of everything thinglike regressed to the subjectivism of the pure act. It hypostatized the indirect as direct. Pure immediacy and fetishism are equally untrue.[16]

Would there be some less troubling way to conceptualize what a non-regressive overcoming of the subject-object dualism might look like? Adorno, who always

insisted on the importance of utopian thought as a negation of the status quo even as he argued against the possibility of fleshing out its contours, could only allude very
tentatively to the answer in the next paragraph of 'Subject-Object'. 'If speculation on the state of reconciliation
were permitted,' he cautiously ventured,

> neither the undistinguished unity of subject and object
> nor their antithetical hostility would be conceivable in
> it; rather, the communication of what was distin-
> guished. Not until then would the concept of communi-
> cation, as an objective concept, come into its own. . . .
> In its proper place, even epistemologically, the relation-
> ship of subject and object would lie in the realization of
> peace among men as well as between men and their
> Other. Peace is the state of distinctness without
> domination, with the distinct participating in each
> other.[17]

To put it in slightly different terms, 'peace' is a three-
starred constellation composed of collective subjectivity,
individual subjectivity and the objective world. As
Adorno insisted in *Negative Dialectics*, 'It is not the purpose of critical thought to place the object on the
orphaned royal throne once occupied by the subject. On
that throne the object would be nothing but an idol. The
purpose of critical thought is to abolish the hierarchy.'[18]

With the Frankfurt School's characteristic reluctance to
detail all of the possible ramifications of a utopian image,
Adorno quickly returns in 'Subject-Object' to a critical
consideration of previous attempts to articulate a defensible epistemology. From Kant's positing of a transcendental subject through Husserl's critique of psychologism, the Western tradition has assumed, as Nietzsche was
the first to point out, that what is *immediately* apparent to
consciousness is not the true first principle of reality.
Instead, the constitutive human mind is elevated to the
status of primary cause. The reason, Adorno contends, is

65

primarily ideological: 'The more individuals are really de-
graded to functions of the social totality as it becomes
more systematized, the more will man pure and simple,
man as a principle with the attributes of creativity and
absolute domination, be consoled by exaltation of his
mind.'[19] The idealists' meta-subject, in other words,
should be understood less as an anticipation of the Marxist
Humanist collective subject of the future than as the inverse image of the totalizing power of the administered
world. It is for this reason that the category of totality,
celebrated by Lukács and other Western Marxists as a
normative goal, was for Adorno 'not an affirmative but
rather a critical category. . . . A liberated mankind would
by no means be a totality.'[20]

But even though an ideology, the postulate of constitutive meta-subjectivity producing such a totality was
no more than an illusory hypostasis of individual subjects.
For as Adorno then argues, what it reflects is not only the
oppressive power of the current totality, but also a more
long-standing social reality. In Adorno's words, 'What
shows up faithfully in the doctrine of the transcendental
subject is the priority of the relations – abstractly rational
ones, detached from the human individuals and their relationships – that have their model in exchange.'[21] Because
the empirical subject is the product of these relations and
not their presupposition, there is a moment of descriptive
truth in the idealist claim of a constitutive meta-subjectivity, even if it is in distorted form.

Although only briefly suggested in 'Subject-Object', the
importance of the exchange principle for Adorno's
negative dialectics would be difficult to exaggerate. His
understanding of it was derived in part from Marx's classical analysis of the exchange value of commodities in capitalism, which is contrasted with their use value to consumers and the value *per se* contributed by the labour of their
producers. Commodities in the capitalist mode of production must be exchanged according to some abstract
medium of equivalence, which is money. Through a pro-

cess of alienation and fetishism, the qualitative differences among various commodities, both in terms of their usefulness to specific consumers and the creative contribution of their specific producers, are neglected in favour of a purely quantitative and abstract measurement of their fungible worth in the market place. And from another perspective, what are originally socially mediated relations among men and between them and the natural world are mystified into merely objective relations among things. This mystification is particularly pernicious because hidden behind the apparent equivalence of the exchange process are real inequalities, which create capitalist surplus value. Adorno stands fast with Marx in asserting that, 'As the principle of exchange, by virtue of its immanent dynamics, extends to the living labours of human beings it changes compulsively into objective inequality, namely that of social classes.'[22]

Adorno, however, differed from Marx, or rather the young Marx, in his explanation of the ultimate source of the exchange process. Rather than emphasizing the genetic role of alienated and abstracted labour in creating a world of commodities whose human origins were forgotten, the premise of that view of reification we saw him criticizing a moment ago, Adorno insisted on an even earlier origin. Following his friend Alfred Sohn-Rethel, whom he credited in *Negative Dialectics* with the insight that abstract thought was a function of the abstraction of the market place,[23] he located the 'original sin' in the division of mental from manual labour. This division he then related to the subject's separation from and domination of the object:

Abstraction – without which the subject would not be the *constituens* at large at all, not even according to such extreme idealists as Fichte – reflects the separation from physical labour, perceptible by confrontation with that labour. When Marx, in his critique of the Gotha Programme, told the Lassalleans that in contrast to the

67

customary litany of popular socialists labour was not the sole source of social wealth, he was philosophically . . . saying no less than that labour could not be hypostatized in any form, neither in the form of diligent hands nor in that of mental production. Such hypostasis merely extends the illusion of the predominance of the productive principle.[24]

Adorno's hostility to the privileging of production in vulgar Marxism, which merely repeated the subject's domination of the object, extended to the concept of reification employed by not so vulgar Marxists like Lukács. Although at times in his own work an apparently Lukácsian usage did appear,[25] reification for Adorno was not equivalent to the alienated objectification of subjectivity, the reduction of a fluid process into a dead thing. Instead, and here Adorno's debt to Nietzsche on the origin of exchange was particularly evident, reification, when he used it in a pejorative sense, meant the suppression of heterogeneity in the name of identity.

Even when Adorno contended, in a widely quoted phrase, that 'all reification is a forgetting',[26] he did not mean that its overcoming would follow from the anamnestic recovery of an original meaning, the reunification of a subject with its lost objectification. Unlike Marcuse, whose concept of memory drew on Hegel's defence of *Erinnerung* as the reinternalization of something externalized, Adorno followed Benjamin in stressing the redemptive power of *Gedächtnis*, the reverential recollection of an object always prior to the remembering subject.[27]

The reversal of forgetting that Adorno wanted was thus not the same as the 're-membering' of something dismembered, the recovery of a perfect wholeness or original plenitude. It meant rather the restoration of difference and non-identity to their proper place in the non-hierarchical constellation of subjective and objective forces he called peace.

Another way to make sense of Adorno's heterodox use of reification is to focus once again on the relationship between subjects and objects, especially natural objects. Reification was not merely a relationship among men, but also one entailing the domination of the otherness of the natural world. Through the kind of conceptual imperialism that Adorno discerned in both positivism and idealism, the natural world was reified into quantitatively fungible fields for human control and manipulation. It was therefore wrong to follow historicist Marxists like Lukács and Gramsci in simply privileging history or society over nature as the locus of freedom. Rather than giving priority to one or the other, a negative dialectics played off nature against history or society and vice versa chiasmically.[28] For ending reification in the Hegelian sense used by Lukács would merely foster its perpetuation in the Nietzschean sense employed by Adorno.

Because Adorno was aware of this paradox, he was suspicious of the claim that all reification might be ultimately overcome. In the letter of 29 February 1940, in which he first formulated the idea that 'all reification is a forgetting', Adorno cautioned Benjamin that it was not a matter of 'once again repeating the Hegelian verdict against reification, but rather of a critique of reification, that is, of a disclosure of the contradictory moments that are contained in forgetting. One could also say: of the difference between good and bad reification.'[29] Such a distinction may also have been in Adorno's mind when he wrote several years later in his essay on Aldous Huxley,

Humanity includes reification as well as its opposite, not merely as the condition from which liberation is possible but also positively, as the form in which, however brittle and inadequate it may be, subjective impulses are realized, but only by being objectified.[30]

69

Adorno's surprising defence of some measure of 'good reification' makes sense only if we recognize his assumption that the tyranny of identity, the exchange principle, and the domination of the constitutive subject over both the contingent subject and the object were all essentially synonymous. But conversely, his much more frequent attacks on 'bad' reification means that he was no less hostile to the denigration of any subjective agency, which characterized philosophies ranging from positivism to structuralist Marxism. Thus, in 'Subject-Object', he defended the necessity of some collective meta-subjectivity as one star in the constellation of emancipation against those who would reduce it to nothing more than a hypostasis of contingent and individual subjectivities. However much it could be seen as the reflection of the abstraction of the market place, such meta-subjectivity also had 'its positive aspect as well: society, as prior, keeps its members and itself alive. The particular individual has the universal to thank for the possibility of his existence – witness thought, which is a general relation, and thus a social one. It is not just as fetish that thought takes priority over the individual.'[31] The mistake of idealism was thus to give absolute primacy to the collective over the individual subject, just as existentialists like Kierkegaard had erred by doing precisely the opposite. In both cases, an identity theory replaced that force-field of irreconcilable moments acknowledged by negative dialectics.

Perhaps because the combined pull of both collective and individual subjectivity was in the direction of the subject, Adorno here and elsewhere placed special emphasis on the counter-attraction of the object. To make his case, he drew on the argument of intentionality that had served phenomenologists since Brentano and Husserl so well: 'What is known through consciousness must be something: mediation aims at the mediated. . . . Potentially, even if not actually, objectivity can be conceived without a subject; not so subjectivity without an object. No matter how we define the subject, some entity

cannot be juggled out of it.'[32] The subject, whether understood as transcendental or individual, is thus always
already objective. One promising implication of this
priority is the likelihood that society, not merely as a
collective subject but also in its objective form, will
appear in critically self-reflective cognition. 'Nothing but
the social self-reflection of knowledge obtains for
knowledge the objectivity that will escape it as long as it
obeys the social coercions that hold sway in it, and does
not become aware of them. Social critique is a critique of
knowledge, and vice versa.'[33] Recognizing the socially
objective moment in knowledge did not, however, mean
for Adorno collapsing thought into social being in the
manner of the sociology of knowledge. As he and his
colleagues in the Frankfurt School often warned in their
critiques of Karl Mannheim,[34] truth could not be reduced
to a reflection of what existed in the social totality of the
moment.

For while the 'predominance of the object' did mean a
refusal to acquiesce in the *reductio ad hominem* of
anthropomorphic epistemologies, it never went so far as
to countenance the total liquidation of the subject. As
Adorno continued in 'Subject-Obect', 'Since primacy of
the object requires reflection on the subject and subjective reflection, subjectivity – as distinct from primitive
materialism, which really does not permit dialectics – becomes a moment that lasts.'[35] It is this insistence on the
permanence of some subjectivity, collective and individual, as the precondition for transcending the status quo
that set Adorno apart from structuralist Marxists like
Louis Althusser, as well as from their cousins in the
post-structuralist camp. It also distanced him from
Benjamin, whose 'Medusan gaze', he worried, might turn
man into little more than 'the stage on which an objective
process unfolds'.[36]

In 'Subject-Object', Adorno focused his attention on
another version of the suppression of non-identity, which
he claimed was the dominant threat at that time, 'the

seemingly anti-subjectivist, scientifically objective identitarian thought known as reductionism'.[37] What made it particularly dangerous was its underlying dependence on a 'latent and thus much more fatal subjectivism'.[38] The objective realism of scientific and positivist thought was in fact constituted by a particular form of subjective rationality, which was projected on to the objective world and then, through a process of reification, forgotten. This seemingly paradoxical assertion can only be understood if we pause for a moment with the concept of 'subjective reason' developed by Adorno and his colleagues.

Drawing on the idealist distinction between *Vernunft* and *Verstand,* Horkheimer and Marcuse in particular had emphasized the 'eclipse'[39] of the former in the modern world in favour of the latter. Whereas *Vernunft* meant a substantive rationality in which the antinomies of thought and existence were reconciled, *Verstand* accepted them as inevitable realities in an unchangeable world. Related to this reduction of rationality to *Verstand* was its instrumentalization, the confinement of reason to the choice of means rather than ends, or in Max Weber's celebrated terms, the hegemony of purposive over value rationality. The ultimate source of this reduction, the Frankfurt School speculated, lay in man's struggle with nature, a struggle aimed at self-preservation. In order to survive, man was compelled to develop skills of manipulating the external world for his own subjective purposes. Taken to an extreme, this subjective, instrumental rationality led to a repression of those aspects of the human personality that were obstacles to the preservation of the self, most notably man's yearning for sensual gratification without infinite delay. It also resulted in the domination of external nature that was the unintended cost of the dialectic of enlightenment, broadly understood. The Frankfurt School, however, did not contend that enlightenment was entirely repressive or that instrumental reason should be completely rejected. As Horkheimer put it in *Eclipse of*

Reason, the aim of critical philosophy was not simply to play objective, substantive rationality off against its subjective, instrumental opposite, but rather to 'foster a mutual critique and thus, if possible, to prepare in the intellectual realm the reconciliation of the two in reality'.[40]

Adorno, it bears repeating, was far less hospitable in 'Subject-Object' and elsewhere to models of perfect reconciliation than those of his Frankfurt School colleagues closer to Lukács's Hegelian reading of Marxism. His uneasiness with the totalizing claims of *Vernunft* has already been noted. But he was at one with the other Critical Theorists in his fear that an increasingly one-sided imbalance between the two types of rationality had characterized the modernization process. The apparently objectivist bias of positivist thought in fact covertly expressed the growing triumph of subjective rationality, whose image of the natural (and human) world as a realm of dead exteriorities open to instrumental manipulation masked the fact that this view of the world was a human construct. Against this illusion, Adorno insisted that

> the object is no more a subjectless residue than what the subject posits. The two contradictory definitions fit into each other: the residue, with which science can be put off as its truth, is the product of their subjectively organized manipulative procedures.[41]

Rather than adopt such procedures based on the ideological suppression of their roots in subjective rationality, a more emancipatory epistemology would approach the object in a different way. In his essay, Adorno described this alternative in terms that show his distance not only from positivism, but also from its Hegelian Marxist antithesis:

> Approaching knowledge of the object is the act in which the subject rends the veil it is weaving around the object. It can do this only where, fearlessly passive, it

73

entrusts itself to its own experience. . . . The subject is the object's agent, not its constituent; this fact has consequences for the relation of theory and practice.[42]

Precisely what these consequences were Adorno did not spell out in 'Subject-Object', nor did he do so very successfully elsewhere either. The only clue to a possible answer in this essay is his fleeting exhortation to trust in a 'fearlessly passive' way one's own experience. In his vocabulary, the term 'experience' had, in fact, a very privileged place, which we must examine before concluding our discussion of 'Subject-Object'. According to one commentator,[43] it, rather than class consciousness in Lukács's sense, was the counter-concept to reification. In certain contexts, such as his dispute with Popper,[44] he employed experience in an apparently neo-Idealist manner as the antidote to empirical methods of verification or falsification. Knowledge, he argued in these instances, was a process of self-reflection dependent on the conceptual mediation of the given. There is thus an inevitable circle in which apparently immediate sense experience is mediated by theoretical concepts, which in turn are founded in and judged by sense experience.

Elsewhere in his work, however, Adorno used experience in a much more unusual way which drew heavily on Benjamin's non-Hegelian critique of the Kantian reduction of experience to its scientific variant.[45] In a now celebrated distinction, Benjamin had divided experience into *Erfahrung,* the integration of events into the memory of collective and personal traditions, and *Erlebnis,* the isolation of events from any such meaningful context, communal or individual. Exemplified by the erosion of the story-teller's ability to weave a coherent tale because of the replacement of narrative by disconnected information in our daily lives, *Erfahrung* had been steadily supplanted by the meaningless incoherence of *Erlebnis* in the culturally impoverished world of late capitalism.[46] Adorno shared his friend's hostility to *Erlebnis,* a term which had been extolled by the irrationalist 'philosophers of life' in Germany because of its alleged spontaneity and freedom from overly intellectual reflection. More recent thinkers like the existentialists were no less guilty of privileging a pseudo-immediacy through what Adorno called their 'jargon of authenticity'. In both cases, a philosophy that wanted to break through the stultifying confines of rationality and tradition to grasp human existence in its naked form had unwittingly duplicated the irrationality and uprootedness of modern social experience.

The antidote to this situation was not, however, a return to the Hegelian idea of a coherently rational history, the objectification of a constitutive meta-subject. Adorno, as we have seen, rejected the Hegelian model of memory as *Erinnerung,* or re-membering what had been sundered, in favour of something closer to Benjamin's *Gedächtnis. Erfahrung,* as Benjamin understood it, was grounded, to be sure, in memory, but not one comparable to that 'epic' restoration of a perfect continuity between past and present defended by historicists and vulgar Marxists alike. Instead, a liberating historical consciousness would explode the continuum of history, brushing it against the grain to redeem memories long repressed. These were memories, however, of something very different from the initial act of subjective creation that Lukács with his Hegelian-Marxist theory of reification had wanted to restore. What they were instead was revealed in Benjamin's highly idiosyncratic philosophy of language,[47] which had a much more profound impact on Adorno's version of Critical Theory, with its special emphasis on experience, than on that of any other member of the Frankfurt School.

One of the essential assumptions of Benjamin's linguistic speculation was that language was rooted in a mimetic experience of the natural world, the capacity to reproduce non-sensuous similarities between self and natural other. It was the continued, if threatened potency of these original similarities that allowed Benjamin to believe that one

could unravel the riddles of the world through attending
to its smallest details in which something of an ur-truth
was unwittingly preserved. But this task was becoming
increasingly difficult as man's mimetic faculty was losing
its potency in the modern world. Although in his more
optimistic moods Benjamin may have felt that film could
help to regenerate it, his essential attitude towards the
contemporary state of language was far from hopeful. The
gap between signifiers and signifieds, which linguists like
Saussure had valorized as an inevitable aspect of all
language, was for Benjamin a falling away from a prelapsarian state of mimetic unity between word and thing.
It was for this reason that he saw allegory with its honest
registering of man's fallen linguistic state as a superior
aesthetic device to classical or romantic symbolism, which
pretended that a unity could now be achieved in art, if not
life. Until a redeemed mankind re-entered a state of grace
in which words once again were similar to the things they
named, memory would have to struggle to rescue the
remnants of the original mimesis or that still experienced
in early childhood, while at the same time resisting the
illusion of its current possibility.

Adorno was always less explicitly attracted to theology
than Benjamin, and seems never to have put much faith in
an original Adamic unity of name and thing. But he
nonetheless shared his friend's concern for a type of experience that would recapture the proper mimetic relationship between man and nature. He understood this
possibility essentially in aesthetic terms, which he interpreted more individualistically than Benjamin. As early as
his critique of Kierkegaard, whose subtitle was 'construction of the aesthetic', Adorno had emphasized the need to
rescue aesthetic experience from those who would render
it inferior to science, religion or philosophy. Its importance lay in its implicitly materialist acknowledgment of
the priority of the object to the subject. In art, unlike
more theoretical activities, conceptual domination of the
natural world was checked by sensuous receptivity.

Although Adorno was always careful to warn against the simple conflation of negative dialectics, with its reflective moment, and aesthetic experience, the two were highly complementary in his thought. One crucial element that they shared was hostility to a communicative notion of truth as an intersubjective construct, which has more recently been defended by Adorno's student, Habermas. Benjamin had vigorously argued that language was not originally a medium of communication between minds that existed prior to their immersion in language. Words that merely communicate thoughts, he contended, are due to the fall of language from its perfect state of mimetic unity between word and thing. If there is anyone with whom communication takes place in that prelapsarian condition, it is God.[48] Although Adorno was less prone to speculate about conversations before the Fall than Benjamin, he did absorb his friend's hostility to intersubjective communication and the restoration or achievement of shared meanings. It was for this reason that he argued in *Negative Dialectics* that

> the concept of sense involves an objectivity beyond all 'making': a sense that is 'made' is already fictitious. It duplicates the subject, however collective, and defrauds it of what it seemingly granted.[49]

The task of philosophy, he contended, was the interpretation of the intentionless content of a reality irreducible to the meaning invested in it by the human subject or by a community of subjects. As he wrote in one of his earliest essays,

> Authentic philosophic interpretation does not meet up with a fixed meaning which already lies behind the question, but lights it up suddenly and momentarily, and consumes it at the same time. . . . Interpretation of the unintentional through a juxtaposition of the real by the power of such interpretation is the programme of

every authentically materialist knowledge, a programme to which the materialist procedure does all the
more justice, the more it distances itself from every
'meaning' of its objects and the less it relates itself to an
implicit, quasi-religious meaning.[50]

With Adorno, we are clearly a long way from those
hermeneutic philosophies that see man, in Weber's
celebrated phrase, as an 'animal suspended in webs of significance he himself has spun'.[51] The memory he valorized in
Erfahrung was very different from the hermeneutics of recol-
lected meaning that Paul Ricoeur identified as the opposite of
a hermeneutics of suspicion.[52] Although Adorno was
certainly closer to the latter, indebted as he was to its three
masters named by Ricoeur -- Marx, Freud and Nietzsche -- he
did not entirely give up a utopian hope for the restoration of
something lost, or better put, of the possibility of something
that might be gained in the future. It was for this reason that
he could still talk in 'Subject- Object' of 'consequences for the
relation of theory and practice'.

Denying the possibility of intersubjective communica-
tions in favour of aesthetic experience, which was
essentially individual, does not, however, suggest a very
plausible programme for realizing Critical Theory's utopian potential. Remaining 'fearlessly passive' in one's
epistemology may be understandable as a defence against
conceptual imperialism, but it is hardly a formula for
political activism. Adorno, however, was never content
with the implication that critical thought, like aesthetic
experience, need remain entirely individual and isolated,
at least in the long run. In another essay published shortly
before his death entitled 'Resignation',[53] he excoriated
those who demanded a perfect unity of theory and
practice in the present and refused to accept their charac-
terization of his position as a covert capitulation to the
status quo. Critical Theory, he maintained, was a sign of
resistance; even though it might one day be apparently
forgotten or suppressed,

it cannot be denied that something of it survives. For thinking has the momentum of the general. What has been cogently thought must be thought in some other place and by some other people. This confidence accompanies even the loneliest and most impotent thought.[54]

In 'Subject-Object', a similar claim accompanied Adorno's final reflection on the implications of transcendental subjectivity:

The concept of transcendentality reminds us that thinking, by dint of its immanent moments of universality, transcends its own inalienable individuation. The antithesis of universal and particular, too, is both necessary and deceptive. Neither one exists without the other – the particular only as defined and thus universal; the universal only as the definition of something particular, and thus itself particular. Both of them are and are not. This is one of the strongest motives of non-idealist dialectics.[55]

If, however, thought is already both universal and particular, collective and individual, and if subjects can be shown to harbour within themselves objectivity and vice versa, and if theory is already a kind of practice, then it might well be asked why was Adorno so extraordinarily critical of the existing state of things? The final, cryptically argued paragraphs of 'Subject-Object' hint at the likely answer. There is, Adorno suggests, a paradox revealed by the subject's reflection on the social sources of its own formalist reflexivity: society may be the ultimate ground of our collectively constructed mental universe, as Durkheim argued, but the arguments Durkheim used to make his case presupposed the very non-constructivist objectivity his own theory denied. The necessity imposed on cognition reflects the 'subject's objective imprisonment in itself'.[56] Yet the objective quality of the constraints that

79

limit possible cognition must not be absolutized, for to do so would be to make any change in the current version of the collective subject impossible. The insight that cognition is at least originally dependent on such collective subjects is valid, despite the argument of nominalists that the individual is always ontologically prior to the whole. For individuation is an historical achievement, not a natural given. 'Man is a result,' Adorno writes, 'not an *eidos* [Husserl's term for the essence of individual objects].'[57] But in the future, Adorno implies, a different kind of cognition, freed from the constraining power of collective subjectivity in its objectified form, may be possible. When that occurs, the liberating potential of transcendental subjectivity will be realized because it will no longer be experienced in the form of an objective constraint. Likewise, the genuinely particularized individual will replace the pseudo-individual of modern mass society as one moment in the force-field of peace. And most utopian of all, the object will once more regain its rightful place alongside the individual and collective subject in a dialectic of mutually supportive non-identity.

The final sentence of 'Subject-Object' refers to a major philosophical position that is unable to account for the reasons why this vision has been thwarted in the past and continues to be in the present. 'Nominalism', Adorno concludes, 'denies society in concepts by disparaging it as an abbreviation for individuals.'[58] That society is more than the mere aggregation of its component members, although not a permanent ontological entity hovering over them, was one of the central assumptions of Adorno's thought, as it was of virtually all Marxists, Western or otherwise. But unlike many in that tradition, Adorno did not privilege the economic dimension, the mode of production, in his attempt to conceptualize the whole. In the twentieth century, he contended, it was necessary to give equal weight to psychological, cultural and generically social factors. Rather than write a new critique of political economy, the major ideology of the classical capitalist era, it was more important to attempt critiques of late bourgeois theories in those other areas instead. As we have seen, Adorno's more strictly philosophical writings always led him outside the realm of pure thought. It is now time to follow his path more closely and investigate the ways in which his reflections on the intellectual traditions of his day were rooted in a fundamental critique of the society which spawned them.

3. The Fractured Totality: Society and the Psyche

'Denn nichts als nur Verzweiflung kann uns retten.'[1]
CHRISTIAN DIETRICH GRABBE

If orthodox Marxism raised the economy to the status of an independent variable over all other spheres of the totality, it was not solely because its theory reflected the economistic 'trade-union consciousness' of an increasingly integrated working class. Classical and neo-classical economists in the nineteenth century were, after all, no less confident of their ability to isolate and fathom the inner workings of a self-regulating economic order. Although, in retrospect, these schools of thought may seem misguided in their over-emphasis on the primacy and autonomy of the economic, at the time when they were writing, the dramatic increase in the industrial forces of production and the no less striking spread of the market relations of production made such an assumption eminently plausible. What Karl Polanyi once called 'the great transformation' did, for a while, produce the illusion that the prime mover of human reality was the newly discovered system of economic laws, which could be observed and mastered with essentially the same tools that had been so helpful in making sense of their natural counterparts.

That most twentieth-century intellectuals, Marxist and non-Marxist alike, have overcome this illusion is due less to their superior perspicacity than to the change in the reality they endeavoured to understand. For in our own time, the dependence of the economy on other aspects of the totality – political, social, cultural, psychological – has become too obvious to ignore. And concomitantly, the

82

nineteenth-century faith in the universal applicability of the scientific method has been widely shaken, save among the narrowing circles of recalcitrant positivists. In the specific tradition of Western Marxism, in which Adorno can be generally situated, the impact of these changes has been registered in different ways. Most fundamentally, the Western Marxists recognized that Marx had actually written a *critique* of political economy rather than merely a rival economic theory. Insofar as critique is a term with roots in German Idealism,[2] the philosophical rather than purely scientific dimensions of Marx's work have come to the fore. Not the least of the reasons for this shift was that it enhanced the role of radical intellectuals in the revolutionary process, for only men with a certain level of education would be able to interpret the esoteric implications of that philosophy to the masses.

No less significant was the recovery of the specifically political dimension of Marx's thought, a recovery whose most important stimulus was the Russian Revolution, which the early Western Marxists understood, in Gramsci's famous phrase, as a revolution 'against *Das Kapital*' with its fetish of the economic. Although most Western Marxists sooner or later left their enthusiasm for Leninism behind, the importance of the Bolshevik restoration of the 'primacy of the political' cannot be overestimated in understanding their liberation from nineteenth-century economism. A new insistence on the centrality of *praxis*, however it might be understood, was shared by virtually all figures in the Western Marxist tradition.

The other alternatives to the privileging of the economic discovered by Western Marxists had somewhat more troublesome implications for the revolutionary project. A new emphasis on a distinctly social, as opposed to economic, dimension of the totality often meant an awareness of those institutions and practices that resisted conceptualization in strictly class terms, class being normally understood by orthodox Marxists only with reference to the mode of production. Bourgeois sociology, as many commentators have noted, had at least some of its roots in a conservative fear of revolution, both political and economic, which often made it substitute moral for material explanations of social cohesion and seek ways to restore the communitarian (*gemeinschaftlich*) order undermined by the market society (*Gesellschaft*) of the present. Although it would be over-simplified to say that the Western Marxist absorption of sociological themes meant a capitulation to the pessimistic anti-utopianism of the great bourgeois sociologists like Weber, Tönnies, Simmel or Durkheim, their discovery of the intransigence of social institutions that could not be reduced to their relation to the prevailing mode of production meant a growing appreciation of both the complexity of the totality and the source of its resistance to revolutionary transformation. It also meant an openness to the possibility that other social groups besides the proletariat might have radical grievances, which a narrowly focused class theory might ignore. Still, the basic implications of the Western Marxist interest in such essentially conservative social formations as the family or the church were not very encouraging for those who hoped for an imminent revolution.

No less sobering were the lessons to be learned from an investigation of two other aspects of the whole, culture and the individual psyche, which traditional Marxism had tended to neglect. Although Lukács, who is now commonly called the first Western Marxist, carried his messianic cultural expectations with him at least for a while after his conversion to historical materialism in 1918, those who followed came to emphasize far more the ways in which culture could thwart revolutionary hopes. Gramsci's concept of 'hegemony', Horkheimer and Marcuse's 'affirmative culture', Althusser's 'state ideological apparatuses', Lefebvre's 'everyday life' all expressed a new recognition of the ways in which culture, no longer merely a superstructure of the economic base,

could buttress the status quo. Although many discerned
still vital subversive impulses in the cultural realm,
especially in certain forms of art, most recognized that
they were in for what Gramsci had called a long 'war of
attrition' rather than a short one of manoeuvre.

Even bleaker were the implications many Western
Marxists drew from their admission that psychology de-
served a legitimate place in making sense of the totality of
human relations. Despite the attempts to arrange a revolutionary shotgun marriage between Marx and Freud by
Wilhelm Reich and Herbert Marcuse, many Western
Marxists came to acknowledge the irreducible tensions
between the two. But what made it impossible to reject
psychology was the unexpected rise of an irrationalist
mass politics in fascism, which was unforseen by orthodox
Marxists. Even after its collapse, the psychological im-
pediments to emancipation could no longer be ignored by
radical analysts of the manipulated society of mass consumption that seemed to follow in its wake. Symptomatic
of the sobering effects of psychoanalysis on Western
Marxist thought was Althusser's use of Lacan to contend
that even after a successful revolution, ideology would
inevitably remain an obstacle to undistorted consciousness.

If we now turn to Adorno's particular reconceptualiza-
tion of post-economistic Marxism, its somewhat idiosyncratic character becomes quickly apparent. Although he
shared in the typical Western Marxist rediscovery of the
dialectical, critical moment in Marxist philosophy, the
Nietzschean and Benjaminian motifs in his thought prevented him from embracing the Marxist Humanist conclusions reached by Lukács, Gramsci and Korsch. As we saw
in the previous chapter, negative dialectics was far more
than another version of left Hegelianism, whose inclina-
tion towards identity theory Adorno vigorously contested.
No less heterodox was his attitude towards the new political emphasis in twentieth-century Marxism. Although he
paid lipservice to the importance of praxis and was

85

certainly no friend of the productivist bias of orthodox Marxism – indeed, Marx himself, according to Adorno, had wanted to turn the world into a 'giant workhouse'[3] – he nonetheless was so fearful of the instrumentalization of theory that he had little of real interest to say about politics. There was, in fact, no sustained discussion of the public sphere, bourgeois democracy, the state or political organization in his work. Although he often implicitly drew on the arguments of other Institute members who did treat these issues, his own interests clearly lay elsewhere. Nor was there any reverence for the political as the realm of freedom that one finds in others of his generation like Hannah Arendt, who was to be so influential on Habermas. Although Adorno staunchly rejected the accusation that he was really an apolitical aesthete, it is hard to avoid the conclusion that there was what many of his German critics liked to call a 'political deficit' in his theory. For when Adorno spoke of power, it was almost always in terms of a pervasive and diffuse domination that transcended any identifiable political realm.[4]

Adorno's real interest lay more in those other areas of the totality that are known as culture, society and the human psyche. In examining his analyses of them, we must, however, be aware of the fact that he respected no watertight disciplinary boundaries. In his own enormously versatile work, he was a virtual microcosm of the Institute's collective staff, which was devised to overcome the compartmentalization of normal academic life. As we saw in the previous chapter, his philosophical speculations always drew him towards society. So, too, when he wrote on cultural, social or psychological matters, the discourse traditionally confined to another discipline would inevitably intervene. In fact, however much he may have moved away from the orthodox Marxist primacy of the economy, he would frequently remind his readers of its continued importance in a still essentially capitalist world.

And yet, isolating Adorno's specific contributions to discrete areas of inquiry may be at least partly defensible.

For although he, like other members of the Frankfurt School, practised a kind of interdisciplinary research grounded in an all-encompassing Critical Theory, he adamantly opposed those kinds of overly harmonistic methodologies that sought to efface all boundaries. In a polemic directed against the neo-orthodox revisionist psychoanalysts Erich Fromm and Karen Horney and the sociologist Talcott Parsons,[5] Adorno insisted on the ideological dangers of overcoming in thought what was still split in reality, the antagonism between universal and particular. Until the actual division of labour was transcended, the scientific division could not be either. As a result, 'The separation of sociology and psychology is both correct and false. False because it encourages the specialists to relinquish the attempt to know the totality which even the separation of the two demands; and correct insofar as it registers more intransigently the split that has actually taken place in reality than does the premature unification at the level of theory.'[6]

Beyond his fear of a premature unification, there also lurked Adorno's sympathy for non-identity as an end itself. Thus, the current incommensurability of different scholarly discourses, although not to be rigidly naturalized, could nonetheless be seen as 'correct' in another way as well: as the distorted anticipation of a non-antagonistic, but still heterogeneously pluralized future. The micrological method that he inherited from Kracauer and Benjamin, which was never fully reconciled with the holistic emphasis he absorbed from Lukács, was thus not merely a temporary expedient appropriate only to this current fallen world of fragmentation. Like Ernst Bloch, Adorno saw such fragments as prefigurations or traces (*Spuren*) of a possible utopia.[7]

One way to pay attention to the particular, although not the only one, was to resist the over-socialization of the individual, whose psychological dimension had not been totally obliterated. Adorno's defence of a necessary psychological moment in any negatively dialectical theory

87

of the totality put him at odds with a well-entrenched tradition in German philosophy that began with Kant's rigorous denunciation of the confusion between the epistemological and empirical subject. In the twentieth century, the most outspoken bourgeois foe of any kind of psychologism was Husserl, who rejected the genesis of the absolute, logical subject in contingent human subjects. Husserl's Marxist counterpart, at least on this issue, was Lukács. Both wanted to defend a version of the trans-cendental, constitutive subject, although in the latter's case it was ostensibly embodied in an historically concrete meta-subject, the proletariat. Adorno's philosophical defence of the contingent, suffering, empirical subject, that ethically materialist moment in his thought we encountered in the previous chapter, led him to argue that psychology (although not psychologism in its reductive forms) was a legitimate bulwark against that subject's suppression in the name of an allegedly higher or more general subject. Here the hedonistic impulse in Critical Theory came to the fore, as Adorno viewed psychology as the best guarantor of the individual's right to genuine corporeal gratification. Whereas the economistic bias of traditional Marxism had identified labour and production as the locus of human freedom, and the philosophical and political bias of Marxist humanism has privileged collective praxis instead, Adorno's emphasis on psychological and sensual pleasure meant he assigned no less significance to the realm of consumption. Although he always remained sceptical of the possibility of achieving real gratification in the present society, a wariness that often gave his writings an ascetic aura, he wholeheartedly endorsed the demand for its ulti-mate realization. In *Dialectic of Enlightenment*, he and Horkheimer emphasized the 'importance of the body'[8] and called for the writing of its underground history in a way that anticipated Foucault. For as Adorno put it in *Minima Moralia*, 'He alone who could situate utopia in blind soma-tic pleasure, which, satisfying the ultimate intention, is intentionless, has a stable and valid ideal of truth.'[9]

As for the traditional philosophical accusation that psychology introduced methods appropriate to the study of natural objects into the very different realm of human subjectivity, that holy sanctum German Idealism called *Geist*, Adorno conceded that this danger did exist. 'If all psychology since that of Protagoras has elevated man by conceiving him as the measure of all things,' he wrote, 'it has thereby also treated him from the first as an object, as material for analysis, and transferred to him, once he was included among them, the nullity of things.'[10] But this reduction was not simply the product of a fallacious method; it reflected instead the penetration of the individual by social reality. 'The dissection of man into his faculties is a projection of the division of labour on to its pretended subjects, inseparable from the interest in deploying and manipulating them to greater advantage.'[11] Even the best psychological theory could not avoid this pitfall: 'Alienating him from himself, denouncing his autonomy with his unity, psychoanalysis subjugates him totally to the mechanism of rationalization, of adaptation.'[12]

That psychoanalysis was, nonetheless, the best psychological theory was evidenced by its resistance to this outcome, especially in its more orthodox and unrevised form. Adorno, who had studied Freud even before he became fully conversant with Marx, came to understand the full ramifications of that resistance only in the 1940s, when the Institute of Social Research began its second massive project on authoritarianism. He was, certainly, always a highly selective disciple. He had, for example, little use for psychoanalytic therapy, which encouraged people to think that their individual fate was really in their own hands. Although he appreciated the rationale for the seemingly cold aloofness of the analyst, he called Freud's central technique of transference 'the artificially contrived situation where the subject performs, voluntarily and calamitously, the annulment of the self which was once brought about involuntarily and beneficially by erotic self-abandonment'.[13] Nor did he accept Freud's resigned valorization of an inevitable and permanent split between society and psyche, even as he spurned the revisionist's attempt to overcome it prematurely. He also found objectionable such aspects of Freud's later theory as the death instinct and maintained a discrete silence in the face of Marcuse's attempt in *Eros and Civilization* to give it a utopian twist. And he was no less hostile to those tendencies in Freud's last writings that led to the conformist ego psychology that seemed to abandon virtually all interest in the instinctual underpinnings of the psyche. For it could only be ideological in the present circumstances to pretend that fully integrated, mature egos might be achieved despite the irrationality of the social whole.

What instead drew Adorno to the early Freud was the way in which his theory unflinchingly registered the traumas of contemporary existence. Telling the harsh truth was itself a kind of resistance to the acceptance of those traumas as inevitable. The more outlandish features of Freud's work were in fact often the locus of such insights, for, as Adorno put it in the frequently cited (itself hyperbolic) remark from *Minima Moralia,* 'In psychoanalysis nothing is true except the exaggerations.'[14] One example of this principle was Freud's notorious argument about female penis-envy, which as a universal condition is nonsense, but as reflection of the present status of women contains a bitter truth. Adorno formulated it in the following terms:

Whatever is in the context of bourgeois delusion called nature, is merely the scar of social mutilation. If the psychoanalytical theory is correct that women experience their physical constitution as a consequence of castration, their neurosis gives them an inkling of the truth. The woman who feels herself a wound when she bleeds knows more about herself than the one who imagines herself a flower because that suits her husband.[15]

90

Similarly, Freud's general emphasis on castration anxiety was more appropriate to the brutal reality of post-liberal capitalism than the model of competing egos posited by his more conformist disciples. 'In the age of the con-centration camp,' Adorno wrote, 'castration is more characteristic of social reality than competitiveness.'[16]

Adorno's sympathy for classical psychoanalysis also de-rived from his recognition that it was produced in an era just before that of the concentration camp, an era when the bourgeois individual had not yet been reduced to little more than an ideology. The emancipatory potential of psychoanalysis was thus intimately linked with the survival of the individual, according to Adorno, who took great exception to efforts, like those of Benjamin, to harness Jung's more avowedly collectivist psychology for radical purposes.[17] In a study of 'Freudian Theory and the Pattern of Fascist Propaganda', written in 1951, he spoke of the 'post-psychological de-individualized social atoms which form the fascist collectivities'[18] and praised Freud's work on group psychology for having foreseen their rise without succumbing to the regressive crowd psychology of Le Bon and others. What made Freudian theory of mass behav-iour superior was its steadfast reliance on an ultimately individualist mode of explanation, which resisted any facile hypostatization of a group mind.

Freud's individual was, to be sure, not without its social side, even if at times it seemed to pit individual against society. Like his Frankfurt School colleagues, Adorno found the psychoanalytic interpretation of the family the critical link between the two levels. The internalization of paternal authority in the bourgeois family, they argued, had provided a role model for the rebellious son, who in turn was able to assert his, admittedly flawed, autonomy in the world. With the invasion of the family by external forces of socialization, such as peer-group pressure and mass culture, and the erosion of the father's economic independence in monopoly capitalism, the child lost the powerful father-figure needed to actualize his own capacity for independence. Although the family, as Fromm had shown, was the transmission belt of bourgeois ideology, it also functioned as what Christopher Lasch later called 'a haven in a heartless world'.[19] In Adorno's words,

> With the family there passes away, while the system lasts, not only the most effective agency of the bourgeoisie, but also the resistance which, though repressing the individual, also strengthened, perhaps even produced him. The end of the family paralyses the forces of opposition. The rising collectivist order is a mockery of a classless one: together with the bourgeois it liquidates the Utopia that once drew sustenance from motherly love.[20]

The nurturant function of the mother, therefore, had been as important as the authority function of the father in instilling a critical capacity in the child. Both were under siege in the modern world, which tended to produce what Adorno and his colleagues called 'authoritarian personalities' instead. Without a strong father-figure both to identify with and rebel against, the sons were left with a submissive attitude towards the diffuse authority of the administered world. Regression to a narcissistic ego rather than progress to an autonomous one was the result, although Adorno foresaw an even worse outcome: 'Narcissism, deprived of its libidinal object by the decay of the self, is replaced by the masochistic satisfaction of no longer being a self, and the rising generation guards few of its goods so jealously as its selflessness, its communal and lasting possession.'[21]

Although this brief summary does not do real justice to the complexity of Adorno's argument, some of its problems may already be apparent. As a number of critics have pointed out,[22] Adorno tended to slight the role of maternal authority in his exclusive emphasis on motherly love, a failing that was partly explained by his relative indifference to pre-Oedipal development. Adorno was also vulnerable for his perpetuation of Freud's male bias, which prevented him from transcending such categories as penis-envy, even if he de-naturalized them. But perhaps the most controversial feature of his appropriation of psychoanalysis was his assumption that the only locus of possible opposition to the status quo was the autonomous male individual produced by the bourgeois family. At least for the foreseeable future, he refused to entertain the possibility of a third alternative other than such increasingly rare survivors of a declining age or the post- psychological, pseudo-individuals of the 'administered world'. And as his critique of ego psychology demonstrated, he was extremely wary of any attempt to posit a healthy individual as a present possibility. 'Every "image of man"', he wrote, 'is ideology except the negative one.'[23] But implied in his own negative image was a somewhat traditional bias, expressed in such remarks as 'totalitarianism and homosexuality belong together',[24] which shows an affinity more with Reich than with the later celebrators of 'polymorphous perversity', Marcuse and Norman O. Brown.

Adorno's understanding of the psychosexual dimension of totalitarianism usually took other forms, but always retained an emphasis on libido. Unlike Fromm who redefined sadism and masochism in essentially non-sexual terms, Adorno insisted on their original psychoanalytic meaning. In *Dialectic of Enlightenment,* he and Horkheimer developed a complicated analysis of the links between anti-Semitism, mass paranoia, projective delusions and repressed homosexuality, which he argued would also help explain the so-called 'ticket mentality'[25] of the postwar era, when the Jews were no longer a viable paranoid target. In fact, the same sado-masochistic tendencies at work in fascism could be discerned in popular culture as well. In all of his analyses of jazz, for example, he endeavoured to show how it expressed 'the mechanical reproduction of a regressive moment, a castration symbolism'.[26]

93

In applying Freud's categories to fascism and mass culture, Adorno always cautioned against assuming that an entirely psychological explanation would suffice, the mistaken assumption made by hasty readers of *The Authoritarian Personality*. As he put it in his essay on fascist propaganda,

> any attempt to understand its roots and its historical role in psychological terms still remains on the level of ideologies such as the one of 'irrational forces' promoted by fascism itself. Although the fascist agitator doubtlessly takes up certain tendencies within those he addresses, he does so as the mandatory of powerful economic and political interests. Psychological dispositions do not actually cause fascism; rather, fascism defines a psychological area which can be successfully exploited by the forces which promote it for entirely nonpsychological reasons of self-interest.[27]

To understand these forces would require an analysis of social reality, which would respect its relative autonomy from other levels of the fractured totality, even as that analysis refused to naturalize the fractures. As we noted earlier, the Western Marxist appropriation of sociological themes often meant a new awareness of the middle-level institutions that resisted conceptualization strictly in class terms. The reverse side of this concern was the fear that such institutions were being radically eroded by the massification of modern society, which also helped weaken the power of economically determined classes. This anxiety was especially prevalent among those of Adorno's fellow émigrés from Germany who had become disillusioned with Marxism after coming to America.

Although there are traces of a mass-society analysis in Adorno's own work, which was deeply sceptical of the survival of intermediate social groups in the 'administered world', he refused to believe that all social articulations were overcome. In 1942, he composed a series of 'Reflec-

tions on Class Theory', which were only published post-
humously in his collected works.[28] In them, Adorno defended the underlying persistence of classes, even if on the
level of subjective consciousness they were no longer
manifest. Both class solidarity and class struggle had
drastically waned, but the fundamental structure of
society remained divided between oppressors and oppressed. In fact, through the extirpation of subjective class
consciousness, so Adorno contended, class society
actually came into its own. For now conformity and false
consciousness had almost completely occluded the revolutionary opposition that would be necessary to undermine the status quo. Believing that the basic structure of
society was mass atomization rather than class division
was thus part of the problem, as were those cultural
analyses that remained on the level of popular or mass
culture. The concept of a 'culture industry' introduced in
Dialectic of Enlightenment was, as we will see in the next
chapter, designed to avoid this latter mistake.

After returning to Germany, Adorno's adherence to
this still basically Marxist analysis did not wane. Although
the Institute as a whole spoke less openly in class terms,
Adorno was as willing to do so as he had been before. In
the essay on 'Society' written in 1965, he insisted that
'although the prediction of increased pauperization of the
proletariat has not proved true over a long period of time,
the disappearance of classes as such is mere illusion,
epiphenomenon. . . . Screened from subjectivity, the difference between the classes grows objectively with the
increasing concentration of capital.'[29] Three years later, he
spoke to the congress of the German Sociological
Association on the issue of 'Late Capitalism or Industrial
Society?'[30] Admitting that contemporary society resisted
conceptualization in uniform categories, as it perhaps had
not during the period of classical capitalism which inspired
Marx's work, he nonetheless contended that in terms of
social relations it must still be understood as capitalist. For
all the dynamism of the forces of production, those rela-

tions had remained essentially static. Men were still dominated by the economy, although the actual dominators were no longer as visible as they had been earlier, a new condition captured in Nietzsche's remark, 'no shepherd and a flock'.[31] The current ruling ideology was the collapse of forces and relations of production into one concept, that of a classless 'industrial society'.

Perhaps the main source of this misguided conflation, at least in methodological terms, was conventional sociology's scientific pretensions, which made a fetish out of recording subjective self-awareness. Attempting to use allegedly objective means to measure the consciousness of social actors, it actually failed to penetrate to the more essential level of objective reality where classes still mattered. Like the bourgeois economists who jettisoned Marx's value theory in favour of marginal utility analysis, positivist sociologists could only register the surface level of the social totality. Although even such methods did reveal some residual class conflict, they were incapable of making sense of the larger workings of society. Indeed, the essential category of society itself always eluded empirical observation, the basis of behavioural social science. 'Because society can neither be defined as a concept in the current logical sense, nor empirically demonstrated,' Adorno argued, 'while in the meantime social phenomena continue to call out for some kind of conceptualization, the proper organ of the latter is speculative *theory*.'[32]

This fundamentally Hegelian argument Adorno defended throughout the 1950s and 1960s when the bulk of his theoretical reflections on society were formulated, often in the heat of combat during the 'positivist dispute' with Popper and his followers. His critique of empiricism never, however, meant a radical rejection of the methods he had grudgingly learned to respect during his American exile. Although his own use of those methods was restricted – he published only one empirical study, using qualitative content analysis, after his return[33] – Adorno opposed those dogmatic dialectical materialists who had no use for positivist 'facts'. 'Hypostatized dialectics', he warned, 'becomes undialectical and requires correction by the fact finding whose interest is realized by empirical social research, which then, in turn, is unjustly hypostatized by the positivistic theory of science.'[34]

Adorno's measured defence of the need for some empirical research was directed not only against rigid dialecticians but also at those German social theorists who were still beholden to the historicist, cultural sciences tradition. The hostility we have noted among idealist philosophers towards psychology was here paralleled by a comparable distrust of sociology, and Adorno wanted no part of either. In several places,[35] he cautioned against turning sociology into a *Geisteswissenschaft,* based solely on the empathetic understanding of *Verstehen.* The assumption that the subjectivity of the observer could re-experience the initial subjective intentionality of historical actors was no more than a secularized version of Hegel's Absolute Spirit returning to itself, and thus a form of subject-object identity theory. What made it particularly inappropriate for contemporary society was the irreducible opacity of the reified aspects of the social whole that were so much like Hegel's 'second nature'. Although society has a subjective side because it always refers back to human beings, it 'is objective because, on account of its underlying structure, it cannot perceive its own subjectivity, because it does not possess a total subject and through its organization it thwarts the installation of such a subject'.[36] Not only was a meta-subject lacking, so too was the individual subjectivity that might account for society on consensual, social contractual lines. Social nominalism of this type was no less ideological than the rigorous social realism that denied any role to individuals whatsoever.

Because the subjective origins of the current social whole were so feeble, it was misleading to assume that social practices could be understood from within as the product of deliberate intentionality. In a world still

97

dominated by the exchange principle and the division of labour, it would be ideological to assume that society was intrinsically meaningful, a text to be read by those with the proper hermeneutic empathy. A sentimental humanist sociology that insisted on treating men, no matter what their actual social conditions, as meaning-giving, creative actors was thus no less misguided than a psychology that sought to honour their allegedly coherent and well-integrated egos. Sociology, as Adorno wanted it to be practised, 'is only peripherally concerned with the ends-means relation subjectively carried out by actors. It is more concerned with the laws realized through and against such intentions. Interpretation is the opposite of the subjective meaning endowment on the part of the knowing subject or of the social actor.'[37]

Thus, whereas on one level empirical methods which objectified men were false, because they purported to be truly objective, but never penetrated beneath the level of reified subjective consciousness, on another level they were true, because they treated contemporary men as the objects into which they had largely been turned in the 'administered world'. Or to put it differently, the truth of positivist methods was their mirroring of the fetishized situation of men in modern society, in which fragmented and unreflected subjective consciousness was divorced from deeper objective trends. Their falsehood lay in their inability to negate and transcend this condition, which only a non-empirical social theory could help to do. Only such a theory could attempt to conceptualize society as a contradictory totality. There were, certainly, ambitious global sociological theories, like that of Parsons, but they were generally classificatory schemes based on greater and greater categorical abstraction from empirical data. There was, however, no way to pass from such data to the theory needed to grasp the whole; Parsons's misguided reconciliation of sociology and psychology was repeated in his ideological attempt to move from facts to grand theories. But, Adorno contended, 'the empirical and the theoretical cannot be registered on a continuum. . . . It is not a matter of smoothing out such divergences and harmonizing them. Only a harmonistic view of society could induce one to such an attempt. Instead, the tensions must be brought to a head in a fruitful manner.'[38]

A dialectical concept of totality must thus recognize its own limitations, a recognition that Adorno had been urging as early as his 1931 address on 'The Actuality of Philosophy'. But it would not abandon its attempt to rise above the one-sidedness of empiricism. For 'society is full of contradictions and yet determinable; rational and irrational in one, a system and yet fragmented; blind nature and yet mediated by consciousness'.[39] How then could theory be sure it was not arbitrarily imposing a construct on a reality that on any level, apparent or essential, was so heterogeneous? Adorno, as we noted in our discussion of his philosophy, never contended that concepts could be perfectly adequate to their objects. Nonetheless, the necessary employment of such imperfect tools was not a mark of theoretical caprice.

The first condition for the construction of the totality is a concept of the object, around which the disparate data are organized. From the living experience, and not from one already established according to the societally installed control mechanisms, from the memory of what has been conceived in the past, from the unswerving consequence of one's own reflection, this construction must always bring the concept to bear on the material and shape it in contact with the latter.[40]

Memory, reflection, and experience (in the sense of *Erfahrung* rather than *Erlebnis*) were all necessary components of theory construction, as was the 'exact fantasy' that Adorno always invoked to justify his critical standpoint.

Being critical meant even undercutting the timeless validity of such dialectical categories as totality, however

99

necessary they were now as a corrective to naive empiricism. In fact, it was the ultimate hope of a negative dialectics to jettison that specific category as an appropriate reflection of social reality. For, as we noted earlier, Adorno insisted that 'a liberated mankind would by no means be a totality'.[41] One might even say that the degree to which totality was a necessary conceptual tool was the degree to which society was still unfree. The answer was not, however, to replace the heteronomous meta-subject with an allegedly autonomous one, as Lukács had argued, and thus achieve a perfectly reconciled community. Totality of any kind was not the goal, but rather 'a thing-in-itself, with all the guilt of reification',[42] a sign of the suppression of non-identity. A utopian social order, to the extent that one dared imagine it from the current realm of necessity, would not be built on the 'myth of total reason' with its totalitarian implications, as one of Adorno's critics claimed he believed.[43] It would instead embody that fluid and delicate balance between substantive rationality and the material needs of the concrete individual which would allow a non-antagonistic, non-hierarchical pluralism to flourish.

Along with the overcoming of the dominating, totalizing rationality of the meta-subject, which appeared in the mistaken fetish of planning among some socialists, would vanish that domination of nature so basic to the dialectic of enlightenment. In its place would be an essentially aesthetic relationship between man and the natural world. As Adorno put it at the end of his 1942 'Theses on Need':

> When classless society promises the end of art, because it overcomes the tension between reality and the possible, it promises at the same time also the beginning of art, the useless, whose intuition tends towards the reconciliation with nature, because it no longer stands in the service of the exploiter's use.[44]

An investigation of precisely what Adorno meant by the aesthetic will have to wait until the next chapter, but it is important to note that the critical vantage point from which he attacked both contemporary society and contemporary sociology was not that of a latterday Hegelian rationalist.

The inappropriateness of reducing Adorno to this position is clearly demonstrated in his refusal to posit an over-arching sociological meta-theory synthesizing all others. His complicated pitting of psychology in general against sociology in general and his critical juxtaposition of social theory against empirical research was replicated in Adorno's analysis of specific theories themselves. Although he did not ignore important figures in the great tradition like Simmel or Mannheim,[45] his major focus was on the dualistic relationship between the tradition's giants, Durkheim and Weber. As elsewhere in his work, for example his analyses of Schoenberg and Stravinsky, Valéry and Proust, and George and Hofmannsthal, he found it illuminating to play one figure off against the other. Rather, however, than searching for a middle ground between them, Adorno pushed the antithetical tendencies of each to their extreme in the hope of exposing the social contradictions underlying their theoretical dichotomy.

In part because of the relative German indifference to Durkheim, Adorno spent more time establishing his importance than Weber's.[46] Among Durkheim's virtues, as he saw them, was a stress on the irreducibility of the social to the psychological, which inoculated sociology against vulgar nominalism. Durkheim's concept of the social as external constraint lacking subjective determination was also true to the actual experience of modern man, whose individual resistance to that constraint had all but vanished. Durkheim, finally, was insightful in his grasp of the inextricable relationship between social 'facts' and morality denied in vain by neo-Kantian or positivist thinkers.

But despite these laudable features, Durkheim's sociology, according to Adorno, must be understood as exhibiting what psychoanalysis called 'identification with

101

the aggressor'.[47] For not only did he correctly identify the suffocating power of the current social whole, he also undialectically reified it as the essence of society *per se*. By privileging only social constraint, objectifying the collective conscience, and seeking to bolster social authority whenever it seemed to sag, Durkheim revealed the basically apologetic function of his thought. Although one might attribute some of this failing to the anxiety of an isolated Jewish intellectual during the Dreyfus Affair, it also expressed the deeper conservative tendencies of most sociology.

In addition, Durkheim's spiritualization of society as a moral community had to be understood as an indication of his covert animosity to man's material needs, just as his emphasis on the irrational nature of social constraint disclosed a certain hostility to rationality that put him closer to his alleged antipode, Bergson, than was normally supposed. Like Freud, although with a less debunking intention, he located the key to modern society in the primitive past, when religious solidarity was the source of a unified social order. Lacking any theory of the genesis of domination in concrete social life-processes, he had no insight into the ways in which it might possibly be overcome through increasing self-consciousness and revolutionary change. Even his vaunted search for a scientific methodology betrayed a conservative bent, because it represented the typical bourgeois defence of irrational ends by instrumentally rational means, a failing which Adorno also attacked in Simmel with his fetishistic formalism.

Although Adorno's reading of Durkheim was not without its blindspots, especially concerning the latter's defence of intermediate bodies within the social whole and his tempered acknowledgment of the value of individualism, it might be justified by reference to his reliance on exaggeration to reveal the underlying implications of an argument. The same defence suggests itself as well for Adorno's analysis of Weber, whose work was a much more vigorous bone of contention in postwar Germany than Durkheim's.[48] If Adorno praised Durkheim for uniting facts and values, he was concomitantly critical of Weber's influential insistence on their separation. But Weber, on the other hand, had no illusions about re-enchanting the disenchanted world with new values, a project which Durkheim naively thought possible. Methodologically, each figure also needed to be corrected by the other. Although Durkheim's holistic and realist view of society corresponded more accurately to current conditions than Weber's individualist and nominalist alternative, it reified and naturalized those conditions. In contrast, Weber's insistence on purposeful social action as opposed to structural determination could be construed as a critical negation of the status quo, even though he often reduced purposes to technical rationality. Similarly, Weber's complicated use of *Verstehen* was less applicable to the administered world than Durkheim's insistence on the thing-like nature of social facts, but it contained an implicit protest against that situation which Durkheim's did not. Weber was also inherently more critical than Durkheim in his search for the rational side of social life. Although he interpreted such rationality in narrowly instrumental and formalist terms, at least he did not capitulate to the authority of the irrational collectivity in the manner of his French counterpart. In fact, Weber's sober analysis of the ambiguities of the rationality whose progress he charted, his celebrated acknowledgment that the 'light cloak' of technological and bureaucratic rationalization had turned into an 'iron cage'[49] provided a useful corrective to the essentially ahistorical sociology of Durkheim, as well as to the facilely optimistic historicism of orthodox Marxism. As we shall see, Adorno's own understanding of the impact of this process on music owed a great deal to Weber's pioneering attempt to extend the concept of rationalization to that art form.

In short, for Adorno, Weber was a necessary corrective to Durkheim, just as Durkheim helped set right the deficiencies in Weber. As Adorno once wrote to Benjamin with reference to a very different opposition, that between high and low art, 'Both are torn halves of an integral freedom, to which however they do not add up.'[50] What prevented them from coming together in a totalized way was the object to which they referred, for 'the irrationality of the contemporary social structure hinders its rational unfolding in theory'.[51]

If, as we have earlier contended, Adorno's own theory itself resisted such a totalization, dissolving instead into a tense force-field of unreconciled impulses, then no clearer example of this tendency can be seen than his critical appropriation of the philosophy of history, to which we now turn in concluding our survey of the psychological and sociological dimensions of his negative dialectics. It is perhaps especially fitting to finish in this way because of the link mentioned a moment ago between Weber's theory of rationalization and Adorno's musicology, for Adorno's negative philosophy of history was the common ground underlying his psychosocial as well as his cultural studies, which we will examine in the next chapter.

It is necessary to term Adorno's speculations about the course of history 'negative' because they never cohered into a completely positive image of temporal development. Like Benjamin, he was explicitly hostile to any unilinear, evolutionary time scheme, whether it be the bourgeois idea of progress or the dialectical materialist faith in the inevitability of a socialist future. Instead, he emphasized the still powerful effect of the past in the present, and conversely, he stressed the possibility, however remote, of a future rupture in the continuum of history. The former was expressed in two different ways with opposing valuations. First, the past could reappear in the present in the form of memory, which kept alive the utopian hopes and critical energies of previous generations. But second, it could reappear as the fateful repetition of the 'ever-same' in the guise of the new, the return of the seemingly repressed even amidst apparent enlightenment.

The latter, his far weaker hope in the future, was manifested in those desperate affirmations of utopia that seem so out of place against his far more frequent expressions of bleak despair. Yet for all his celebrated pessimism, Adorno never let himself forget that 'it lies in the definition of negative dialectics that it will not come to rest in itself, as if it were total. This is its form of hope.'[52]

To grasp all of the complexity of Adorno's negative philosophy of history, it is useful to isolate the competing elements that, for analytical purposes, we can identify with the component stars in his intellectual constellation. In his more strongly Hegelian Marxist moments, Adorno tacitly embraced a temporal scheme that in important ways echoed that of Lukács. Not only did he insist on the world-historical importance of the rise and universalization of capitalism, he also conceptualized the highpoint of that process as having occurred in the first half of the nineteenth century, when the bourgeois individual was at his height and the nascent proletariat was just beginning to cohere. He thus often spoke positively about the 'period around 1848, when the class struggle revealed itself as a conflict between a group immanent to society, the middle class, and one which was half outside it, the proletariat'.[53] In philosophical terms, this was roughly the period of Hegel's prominence, when the foundations of dialectical philosophy, both positive and negative, were laid. And culturally, it was the culmination of the age of Goethe, Balzac, and most important of all for Adorno, Beethoven, the figures who represented the triumph of high bourgeois culture before the collapse of the mediated unity of subject and object. During his so-called 'middle period', Beethoven in particular created works of art that were genuine totalities, representing the realized intention of the active subject in objective form. That Adorno, like other Hegelian Marxists, measured the subsequent decline, even 'decadence', of Western culture from that time has been noted by Lukács's former student Ferenc Feher, who as a result calls into question the traditional

105

image of the two thinkers as radical antipodes.[54]

There is a great deal of insight in Feher's revision, but it underestimates the countervailing tendencies in Adorno's philosophy of history. Most obviously, Adorno the aesthetic modernist had a very different evaluation of the course of recent developments than more conventional Hegelian Marxists like Lukács. Rather than evincing scarcely disguised nostalgia for the lost golden age of bourgeois high art, Adorno ruthlessly rejected any calls for the restoration of an allegedly 'healthy' realism or classicism, either in bourgeois or proletarian guise. Indeed, regressions of any kind were always suspect to him as phenomena to be understood as much in psychological as social or cultural terms. With Rimbaud, he insisted that it was necessary to be absolutely modern, at least in terms of rejecting the possibility of innocently reviving older forms. Indeed, even the modernist 'new' music of Schoenberg he so admired could 'grow old'[55] and become the object of inauthentic restoration, as demonstrated by Stravinsky's late conversion to the twelve-tone row. Although there is some truth to the recent charge that Adorno himself did not live up to his injunction and remained beholden to a kind of classical modernism, which was no longer viable after the death of the avant-garde,[56] he nonetheless resisted the more orthodox Hegelian Marxist nostalgia for a lost age of cultural wholeness, whose restoration the revolution would bring about.

Even more drastically at odds with Hegelian Marxism was the temporality derived from what we can call the 'cultural-mandarin-in-crisis' moment in Adorno's force-field. Although in part reminiscent of Lukács because of his respect for the accomplishments of high bourgeois culture in its individualist phase, Adorno, in this mood, was far less inclined to relate them positively to the rise of capitalism, which he identified more with base 'civilization' than real 'culture'. And he was even more reluctant to posit the proletariat as their reviver. Here, that Weberian analysis of the dark side of bureaucratic,

106

instrumental, formal rationality was especially important. So too was Adorno's nuanced distrust of science and technology, which allowed some unfriendly critics to label him a romantic foe of all intellect.[57] The *locus classicus* of this tendency in Adorno's thought was *Dialectic of Enlightenment,* which places the major break in the West with the first division of labour, the separation of subject from object, and the initial domination of nature, that is, well before the rise of capitalism. Here the commodity form of capitalism is seen as subordinate to these earlier events, which seem to culminate with fateful inevitability in the revenge of abused nature that is fascism.

With a bitterness more characteristic of the right-wing purveyors of cultural despair than their leftist opponents, Adorno and Horkheimer detailed the unexpected consequences of a rationalization that purported to supplant mythic thought, but in fact helped to repeat it. The implications of this 'retrogressive anthropogenesis',[58] as one commentator called it, was apparent in the widely quoted lament in *Negative Dialectics* that, 'No universal history leads from savagery to humanitarianism, but there is one leading from the slingshot to the megaton bomb.'[59] Taken as the sole representation of Adorno's philosophy of history, this remark has led one critic to conclude, 'What was criticized in Marx as an apotheosis of history is transformed by Adorno into a "diabolization" of history. What was condemned in Hegel is once more turned on its head: radical evil – Evil as such – is promoted to the status of the World Spirit. The history of salvation is replaced by the history of damnation.'[60]

Although justifiable in part, this argument is also too one-sided in the light of Adorno's other temporal schemes. The religious language in this citation suggests the source of one of them, the Jewish component in Adorno's thought. Here two contradictory implications can be discerned. Insofar as Adorno was deeply affected by his ruminations on the Holocaust, Auschwitz functioned for him as an historical nodal point of the kind

107

usually reserved for messianic interventions into history. It was, of course, a reverse messianism, that of the devil rather than God, which allowed him to speak of 'after Auschwitz' with almost the same portentousness that a Christian would speak of AD. In this sense, history was not a gradual decline into hellishness, but displayed instead the ability to break dramatically with the course it had been following and open itself up to something radically different, a possibility made even more threatening by the lesson of Hiroshima. But by the same token, such a messianic incursion could have its benign side, the redemptive moment that Benjamin had cherished and Adorno never fully abandoned.

Finally, there is even a proto-deconstructionist element in Adorno's negative philosophy of history that is perhaps due to a shared indebtedness to Nietzsche. Not only was Adorno suspicious of any original moment of plenitude now lost or forgotten, he was also highly sensitive to the repetitions that cut through dialectical development or cultural decline. As early as his 1932 paper on 'The Idea of Natural History',[61] he juxtaposed the stasis of nature with the dynamism of history, using one to undermine the primacy of the other. Even in his discussions of modernism, he was deeply aware of the return of the archaic in new forms, the 'naturalization' of what seemed most historical. Not for him was the one-dimensional vision of modernism and modernization as a progressive dissolution of structures, a process in which 'all that is solid melts into air'.[62] As we have seen when examining his defence of the continuing applicability of a class rather than mass-society analysis, he was determined to keep in sight those increasingly hidden, but still potent elements of the dominating totality that ideology sought to mask.

But if Adorno emphasized the current power of the 'ever-same', it was always in the hope of breaking its spell in the future. As he once put it, 'Only he who knows the most recent as the same will serve what is different.'[63] Because of this unrelinquished desire for something genuinely new, Adorno was immunized against the deconstructionist tendency to affirm the current society as already characterized by the indeterminate, carnivalesque, but repetitive play of irreducible differences. As Habermas once noted,

> If one takes Adorno's *Negative Dialectics* and *Aesthetic Theory* seriously and accepts them, and if one then wishes to withdraw just one step from this scene out of Beckett, then one has to become somewhat of a poststructuralist to conceptualize it. Adorno never took this step. He would have considered it a betrayal of the rational heritage of Critical Theory.[64]

Or to put it in terms of his philosophy of history, however Nietzschean it may have seemed, Adorno never succumbed to the belief that recurrence was eternal, let alone affirmed it as necessary and good.

What emerges from these conflicting temporal schemes, then, is Adorno's abiding suspicion that any positive philosophy of history will have regrettable consequences, especially if it becomes a theodicy in which both human initiative and human suffering are cancelled out in the name of a higher law. As he and Horkheimer warned in *Dialectic of Enlightenment*,

> The philosophy of history repeats a process which occurred in Christianity: the goodness which in reality remains at the mercy of suffering is concealed as the force which determines the course of history and ultimately triumphs. It is idolized as the spirit of the world or as an immanent law. . . . Because history as the correlation of unified theory and as something which can be built is not good but horror, so thought is in fact a negative element. Hope for better circumstances – if it is not a mere illusion – is not so much based on the assurance that these circumstances would be guaranteed, durable, and final, but on the lack of

109

respect for all that is so firmly rooted in the general suffering.[65]

But if such hope is to be more than mere illusion, it is not easy to see in Adorno's analyses of psychology or sociology where it can be grounded. There are no specific social forces or structures that embody resistance to the totalizing power of the administered world, nor is there an irreducible psychological substratum that can hold out forever against the increasing interventions of the external society.[66] And, of course, politics, as Adorno saw it, is utterly bereft of any genuinely subversive energies that are not immediately turned into instrumentalized mechanisms for preserving the status quo. Indeed, if any place-holder of redemption can be found outside of Critical Theory itself, it lay for Adorno only in what Stendhal called 'the promise of happiness' that was art. In our final chapter, we must therefore turn to the remarkable efforts he made to detect the faint heartbeat of utopia amidst the deafening cacophony of contemporary culture.

4. Culture as Manipulation; Culture as Redemption

'In dem, was man Philosophie der Kunst nennt, fehlt gewöhnlich eins von beiden: entweder die Philosophie oder die Kunst.'[1]
FRIEDRICH SCHLEGEL

'Culture', as Raymond Williams recently reminded us, 'is one of the two or three most complicated words in the English language.'[2] Although the complications were not precisely equivalent, the same might easily be said of *Kultur*, a word with special resonance in Germany ever since its eighteenth-century juxtaposition to *Zivilisation*.[3] Few twentieth-century intellectuals have been as sensitive to its multiple meanings and contradictory implications as Adorno, who moved from the ambience of German *Kultur* to Anglo-American culture and back again, while all the time feeling deeply estranged from whichever version he encountered.

If, in fact, one had to conjecture the most likely source of Adorno's claim on our attention and that of posterity, it would be his extraordinarily rich and varied writings on culture in all senses of the word. Whereas his contributions to psychology, sociology and perhaps even philosophy were made as a critic of earlier theoretical positions, as an analyst of culture he was more directly engaged with primary material. As a musician and composer, he was able to write about many artistic issues from within. And as his involvement with the writing of Thomas Mann's *Doctor Faustus* illustrates, he could also be more than just a critic of literature. Indeed, it is even possible to say that much of his critical writing itself

111

aspired to the level of art,[4] which is one of the sources of its incommensurability with so much social scientific discourse on the same issues. On occasion, as in the case of *Quasi una Fantasia*,[5] he loosely structured his writing like a musical composition. Anticipating the deconstructionists, with whom he has been compared in this regard,[6] Adorno called into question the very boundary between criticism and creation, without, however, ever effacing it entirely.

To speak of culture means immediately to be confronted by the basic tension between its anthropological and elitist meanings. For the former, which in Germany can be traced back at least to Herder, culture signifies a whole way of life: practices, rituals, institutions and material artifacts, as well as texts, ideas and images. For the latter, which developed in Germany as an adjunct of a personal inwardness contrasted with the superficiality of courtly manners, culture is identified with art, philosophy, literature, scholarship, theatre, etc., the allegedly 'humanizing pursuits' of the 'cultivated' man. As a surrogate for religion, whose importance was steadily eroding, it emerged in the nineteenth century as the repository of man's most noble accomplishments and highest values, often in tension with either 'popular' or 'folk' culture, as well as with the more material achievements of 'civilization'. Because of its undeniably hierarchical and elitist connotations, culture in this more restricted sense has often aroused hostility from populist or radical critics, who allege its natural complicity with social stratification.

Adorno's ruminations on these multiple meanings of culture took many forms. As an émigré in an alien environment, he sometimes assumed the role of a cultural anthropologist intent on reading the unfamiliar practices of his host country. In *Minima Moralia* in particular, he commented, often with remarkable acuity, on everything from zoos to divorce patterns, jogging to insomnia, IQ tests to occultism. At the root of his interest in the larger concept of culture was his insistence on the inevitable intertwining of material and ideal or spiritual reality. To distinguish abstractly between an allegedly disinterested high cultural sphere and baser human interests and needs, in the manner of, say, Kantian aesthetics, was to deny the hedonist moment in all genuine culture, whose sensuous side contained a somatic prefiguration of a more generalized future happiness. To celebrate culture only for its transcendence of material concerns was, furthermore, to undercut the concept's critical potential. As he wrote in an essay on 'Culture and Administration', 'The process of neutralization – the transformation of culture into something independent and external, removed from any possible relation to praxis – makes it possible to integrate it into the organization from which it untiringly cleanses itself.'[7]

The Marxist in Adorno also deeply distrusted any concept of culture that forgot its tainted origins in social inequality. All culture, he insisted, 'ekes out its existence only by virtue of injustice already perpetrated in the sphere of production, much as does commerce'.[8] To isolate culture as something superior to society, free from its constraints, was to ignore the pervasive power of the dominating totality into which modern life had coalesced. In fact, he argued in *Prisms*, 'The greatest fetish of cultural criticism is the notion of culture as such. For no authentic work of art and no true philosophy, according to their very meaning, has ever exhausted itself in itself alone, in its being-in-itself. They have always stood in relation to the actual life-processes of society from which they distinguish themselves.'[9] Indeed, the very hypostatization of the concept of culture as a coherent reality transcending specific works of art was a dangerous development. 'To speak of culture', Adorno and Horkheimer paradoxically contended, 'was always contrary to culture. Culture as a common denominator already contains in embryo that schematization and process of cataloguing and classification which brings culture within the sphere of administration.'[10]

113

But if Adorno insisted with characteristic Hegelian Marxist fervour on the importance of a holistic analysis, which avoided the fetishization of one of the parts, he was equally adamant in his stress on the irreducible contradictions within that whole. The most fundamental of these, as we have already noted, was the split between mental and manual labour, which was at the root of the dialectic of enlightenment. The tension between culture, defined in the elitist sense, and culture as a whole way of life was a product of this division. Overcoming it was one of Adorno's primary desiderata, but he recognized that the solution could never be achieved within culture itself; nor could it come from the collapsing of high culture into the everyday life of the present, which would merely negate it without realizing its emancipatory potential.

A dialectical theory of culture must therefore resist both the abstract dichotomy of culture and material life and the no less abstract denial of their distinction. In an aphorism entitled 'Baby with the bath-water' from *Minima Moralia*, he spelled out his argument:

> Among the motifs of cultural criticism one of the most long-established and central is that of the lie: that culture creates the illusion of a society worthy of man which does not exist; that it conceals the material conditions upon which all human works rise, and that, comforting and lulling, it serves to keep alive the bad economic determination of existence. This is the notion of culture as ideology, which appears at first sight common to both the bourgeois doctrine of violence and its adversary, both to Nietzsche and Marx. But precisely this notion, like all expostulations about lies, has a suspicious tendency to become itself ideology.[11]

The reason for this reversal, Adorno contended, was that too dismissive a concept of culture, which reduced it to a mere ideological reflex of the status quo, did an injustice to the countervailing impulse in high culture at its best.

Culture as Manipulation; Culture as Redemption

Unlike those eager debunkers of culture, both of the right and the left, who reach for their gun whenever they hear the word, Adorno insisted on its critical as well as ideological dimension:

> If material reality is called the world of exchange value, and culture no matter what refuses to accept the domination of that world, then it is true that such refusal is illusory as long as the existent exists. Since, however, free and honest exchange is a lie, to deny it is at the same time to speak for truth: in face of the lie of the commodity world, even the lie that denounces becomes a corrective.[12]

Indeed, for reasons that we will examine shortly, Adorno placed the fault line between works of art he praised and those he damned precisely with reference to where they stood on this issue.

The task of the dialectical cultural critic, then, was neither to celebrate the separation of mind from matter, art from administration, culture from civilization, nor to paper over the splits as if they had not occurred. It was rather to insist on the radical ambiguity of a high culture whose objective content, its promise of happiness, could only be realized with its generalization to culture in the larger sense, while at the same time, its dependence on the material conditions of this and past societies helped thwart that very realization. In other words, the critical energies in the elite concept of culture had to be marshalled against the ideological function of its anthropological counterpart, while the progressive impulses of the latter had to be turned against the conservative implications of the former.

To rescue the emancipatory potential in the fractured cultural reality of our day, according to Adorno, necessitated a complicated method that would combine the two approaches he called immanent and transcendent critique. The former, which had its roots in the hermeneutic tradition of Schleiermacher and Dilthey,[13] began with a recognition that the cultural critic was firmly embedded in the culture he wanted to criticize. As he warned in an article on Mannheim,

> The answer to Mannheim's reverence for the intelligentsia as 'free-floating' is to be found not in the reactionary postulate of its 'rootedness in Being' but rather in the reminder that the very intelligentsia that pretends to float freely is fundamentally rooted in the very being that must be changed and which it merely pretends to criticize.[14]

This rootedness does not, however, mean that the critic has no vantage point from which to question the values of his culture. For immanent critique meant treating them as ideologies which could be compared with the realities of the objective world.

> It takes seriously the principle that it is not ideology in itself which is untrue but rather its pretension to correspond to reality. Immanent criticism of intellectual and artistic phenomena seeks to grasp, through the analysis of their form and meaning, the contradiction between their objective idea and their pretension.[15]

In the mid-twentieth century, however, the ability to exercise such an immanent critique was threatened by what Adorno saw as the diminished role of genuine ideologies in reproducing society. Traditionally, ideologies had been generated by the need to justify a problematic social condition, which was perceived as such. Although apologetic in intent, ideologies also contained a critical impulse in the space between their justifications and the reality they claimed to embody. But the Nazi experience, Adorno lamented, when no one took the content of ideology seriously as more than a tool of manipulation, signalled the collapse of this distance:

Where purely immediate relations of power predominate, there are really no ideologies. . . . Ideology today is the condition of consciousness and unconsciousness of the masses, as objective spirit, not the miserable products which imitate and debase this spirit in order to reproduce it. For ideology in the proper sense, relationships of power are required which are not comprehensible to this power itself, which are mediated and therefore also less harsh. Today society, which has unjustly been blamed for its complexity, has become too transparent for this.[16]

This transparency is itself masked by cultural practices that are unmediated reproductions of the status quo, practices which lack the necessary tension between justification and reality for an immanent critique. 'Nothing remains then of ideology but that which exists itself, the models of a behaviour which submits to the overwhelming power of the existing conditions.'[17] Pitting concept against object in the manner of the Frankfurt School's 'ideology critique'[18] of the 1930s was thus no longer sufficient, if indeed it ever really was.

For if the current whole was entirely 'untrue', then some transcendent point outside of it was necessary to support a genuinely critical theory. Here the capacities we have seen Adorno enlist in his defence of speculative theory against sociological empiricism – imagination, memory, experience – were the source of whatever transcendence he could claim for his own. Adorno, however, never rigorously justified his privileged status beyond talking vaguely of 'a stroke of undeserved luck' that 'has kept the mental composition of some individuals not quite adjusted to the prevailing norms'.[19] It was thus left to his successors in the Frankfurt School tradition, most notably Habermas, to attempt to find a more satisfactory transcendental or quasi-transcendental vantage point for their critique. That Adorno himself seems to have been somewhat uneasy with his solution to the problem is evinced by his insistence that neither immanent nor trans-cendent critique could ever suffice on its own:

> The alternatives – either calling culture as a whole into question from outside under the general notion of ideology, or confronting it with the norms which it itself has crystallized – cannot be accepted by critical theory. To insist on the choice between immanence and trans-cendence is to revert to the traditional logic criticized in Hegel's polemic against Kant.[20]

By whatever means, Adorno was determined to preserve a critical vantage point towards cultural issues, which he felt was severely jeopardized by the empirical approach of mainstream sociologists of culture. Although he came to temper somewhat the hostility to such methods that had undermined his ill-fated collaboration with Lazarsfeld's Radio Research Project,[21] he always contended that, 'Culture is the condition that excludes the attempt to measure it.'[22] As he insisted in his interchange with the empirical sociologist of music Alphons Silbermann, the objective social and aesthetic meaning of a work is not reducible to an external process of communication be-tween a producer and a consumer. Only a theoretically informed investigation of the mediated social relations *within* the cultural artifact itself can illuminate its full significance. As he demonstrated in such studies as his trenchant dissection of the *Los Angeles Times* astrology column,[23] a qualitative content analysis can illuminate the function of a cultural phenomenon without relying on the subjective reactions of its victims. Even the more sophisticated reception-aesthetics of a Hans Robert Jauss was insufficient for Adorno.[24] Although his own aesthetic theory was indebted to Kant, Adorno had nothing but scorn for the tradition of emphasizing subjective or inter-subjective taste that derived from the *Critique of Judgment*, whether it be taste investigated empirically or hermeneutically.

118

Such methods were particularly inappropriate, Adorno contended, when applied to the sphere where they were most frequently used, that of contemporary mass culture. Here in particular, manipulated consciousness could not be taken as the ultimate data of a critical analysis; what had to be understood were the deeper trends that profited from that manipulation. Only through a more direct confrontation with the works themselves could these underlying forces be understood.

Adorno's relentless animus towards mass culture was among his most controversial characteristics, often leading to the charge that he was an elitist snob, an arrogant mandarin, and even (because of his hatred for jazz) a covert racist.[25] These glibly defensive epithets fail to acknowledge the extent to which the very same criticisms he levelled against mass culture were often directed as well against most elite culture, which he refused to fetishize as inherently superior. There are, for example, few aspects of his critique of the cinema that cannot be found in his attack on Wagner, whose operas, contra the young Nietzsche, 'witness the birth of film out of the spirit of music'[26] rather than a resurrected Greek tragedy. And although he may have been overly eager to demonstrate the sado-masochistic core of jazz, he was no less willing to discern the same pathology in the music of Stravinsky.[27] In short, all culture for Adorno, high or low, contained a moment of barbarism.

That Adorno felt especially unsympathetic towards what passed for popular culture is, however, undeniable. Indeed, at times he clearly prejudged its significance, as he later admitted when he confessed his visceral reaction to the very word 'jazz'. But his hostility came less from the conservative mandarin conviction that the revolt of the masses had polluted the temples of culture than from his belief that the culture of the masses was a wholly synthetic concoction cynically imposed on them from above. Rather than cultural chaos or anarchy, the current situation was one of tight regimentation and control. Although Adorno

119

sometimes admitted uncertainty about the calculated, conspiratorial nature of that control, he never doubted the direction of cultural domination. It was for this reason that he and Horkheimer preferred the loaded term 'culture industry' to popular or even mass culture. As Adorno later recalled,

> In our drafts we spoke of 'mass culture'. We replaced that expression with 'culture industry' in order to exclude from the outset the interpretation agreeable to its advocates: that it is a matter of something like a culture that arises spontaneously from the masses themselves, the contemporary form of popular art. From the latter the culture industry must be distinguished in the extreme.[28]

The sources of Adorno's concept of the culture industry, as Andreas Huyssen has pointed out,[29] are to be found in his own experience with the new, technologized, anonymous mass culture of the Weimar era, Nazi pseudo-folk culture and the American popular culture of the 1930s and 1940s. One might add his disillusionment with the proletariat, whose efforts to create an oppositional working-class culture Adorno accounted a complete failure. Unlike his friends, Benjamin, Brecht and Kracauer, he felt little sympathy for the experiments in mass art using modern technological means that had been made by the Weimar left on the basis of Soviet models.[30] Nor was he as optimistic as his friend Bloch about the distorted moment of protest, the utopian traces, in *völkisch* culture (a disagreement that extended as well to their attitudes towards Wagner).[31] And unlike his Frankfurt School colleague Marcuse, who came to see the blues and jazz as critical art forms,[32] he had only contempt for the indigenous forms of popular art he encountered in exile. Eurocentric to the last, Adorno never felt any real sympathy for American, let alone more 'primitive' forms of culture outside of the West. For Adorno, there was no nascent counter-hegemony, as Gramsci would have put it, no resurrected public sphere, as Habermas would have argued, emerging to challenge the total reification of consciousness produced by the culture industry.

Adorno traced its origins as far back as the seventeenth century, roughly the period when the first important controversy over its implications broke out in the writings of Montaigne and Pascal. As Leo Lowenthal has pointed out in his synopsis of their implicit debate,[33] Montaigne defended the healthy role of diversion, which would enable the common man to adapt to increasing social pressures, whereas Pascal, far more concerned with the salvation of man's soul than his terrestrial adjustment, scorned mere entertainment as escapist and demeaning. Adorno, in most respects, was descended from Pascal rather than Montaigne. Unlike the latter, whose resignation about the imperfections of the human condition Adorno (despite his reputation as a pessimist) did not share, he insisted that mass diversions cheated men out of their potential for more valuable and fulfilling activities. But unlike Pascal, Adorno did not identify man's highest state with spiritual salvation; rather he contended that it was genuine corporeal gratification that was denied by the culture industry. Contrary to those critics who saw his position as a covert Puritanism, he claimed that what passed for happiness in the present was a pale imitation of the real thing:

> The culture industry perpetually cheats its consumers of what it perpetually promises. The promissory note which, with its plots and staging, it draws on pleasure is endlessly prolonged; the promise, which is actually all the spectacle consists of, is illusory: all it actually confirms is that the real point will never be reached.[34]

For Adorno, an art that exposed the palliatives of mass culture for what they were, more accurately expressed the pain of modern existence and was thus ultimately on the side of genuine pleasure. 'The secret of aesthetic sublima-

121

tion', he contended, 'is its representation of fulfilment as a broken promise. The culture industry does not sublimate; it represses.'[35]

One of Adorno's chief complaints against the culture industry was its deliberately mystifying function. Here Marx's classic analysis of the fetishism of commodities was at the root of his argument.[36] For Adorno contended that the products of the culture industry were not works of art that were then turned into commodities, but were rather produced *from the very beginning* as fungible items for sale in the market place. The distinction between art and advertising, he claimed, was obliterated, as cultural products were created for exchange rather than to satisfy any genuine need. 'The principle of idealistic aesthetics – purposefulness without a purpose – reverses the scheme of things to which bourgeois art conforms socially: purposelessness for the purposes declared by the market. At last, in the demand for entertainment and relaxation, purpose has absorbed the realm of purposelessness.'[37] Like other economic commodities, their productive origins and functional purposes were masked by a phantasmagoric smokescreen that engendered false consciousness. As Lowenthal put it in a phrase Adorno liked to cite, 'mass culture is psychoanalysis in reverse' because instead of curing authoritarian personalities, it helped spawn them.

Adorno's debt to Marx's analysis was especially apparent in his emphasis on the role of fetishism in the culture industry, which appeared in one of his earliest sociological discussions of music in the 1930s.[38] Whereas at its height, bourgeois music produced total compositions whose aesthetic unity and coherence could be appreciated by attentive listeners, contemporary music, with few exceptions, presented the listener with a disjointed pastiche of unrelated fragments that could not be heard as a meaningful whole. Fetishization, in fact, took many forms in current musical life, such as the cult of star conductors and performers, the obsession with technical perfection in hi-fi equipment, and the impoverished listening of those who can pick out nothing but famous melodies, like second-hand quotations, from the great masterpieces. 'The development of the culture industry', Adorno and Horkheimer argued, 'has led to the predominance of the effect, the obvious touch, and the technical detail over the work itself – which once expressed an idea, but was liquidated together with the idea.'[39]

The underside of the fetishism of music, Adorno contended, was the regression of hearing, which meant a growing inability to concentrate on anything but the most banal and truncated aspects of a composition. The result in popular music was particularly sinister, as listeners were programmed to accept music that eschewed any coherent development and presented instead a spatialized temporality of the 'ever-same', which subtly served to reinforce the status quo as inescapable fate. The seemingly incessant replacement of one fad with another in popular music was really a screen for the reproduction of the same basic relations that underlay the system as a whole. Predigested formulae were replicated ad infinitum to the detriment of any genuine innovation. Even the celebrated improvisatory interludes in jazz, Adorno asserted, followed highly circumscribed patterns.

Another way in which the culture industry functioned, according to Adorno, was to use residues from earlier, more autonomous works of art for its own purposes. Tragedy, for example,

is reduced to the threat to destroy anyone who does not cooperate, whereas its paradoxical significance once lay in a hopeless resistance to mythic destiny. Tragic fate becomes just punishment, which is what bourgeois aesthetics always tried to turn it into. The morality of mass culture is the cheap form of yesterday's children's books.[40]

What Benjamin had called the 'aura' of works of art, their ritually or cultically induced halo of authenticity and

123

uniqueness, had been virtually destroyed by technological reproduction, but the culture industry employed a pseudo-aura to give the effect of individuality to what in fact were totally standardized commodities. The 'jargon of authenticity' in philosophy thus had its correlate in the realm of mass culture. Both masked the actual decline of the bourgeois subject, without, however, signifying the rise of his collective successor. 'Culture is the perennial claim of the particular over the general, as long as the latter remains unreconciled to the former,'[41] but all the culture industry could provide was a pseudo-individualism that masked the power of exchange to undermine the non-identical in the administered world.

It is important to emphasize Adorno's reliance on a still Marxist analysis here to avoid the implication sometimes drawn that he blamed the culture industry more on technological developments than economic ones. Adorno, to be sure, had none of the faith in the emancipatory potential of technology that seems to have inspired Benjamin at times. And his various analyses of new technologies like radio, television, film and electronic music did frequently point to the dominating uses to which these media might easily be put. Indeed, he sometimes spoke as if technology had replaced ideologies as the main mystifying power in modern society. But it would be incorrect to claim that he attributed the culture industry essentially to technology or the mass media *per se.* Although he often talked of a 'technological veil', it was what was behind the veil that most concerned him. 'The basis on which technology acquires power over society', he insisted, 'is the power of those whose economic hold over society is greatest.'[42]

It would be thus more correct to characterize his position by saying that the economic interests of late capitalism were advanced by the substitution of reproductive technology for individual productive 'technique'.

The concept of technique in the culture industry is only in name identical with technique in works of art. In the

latter, technique is concerned with the internal organization of the object itself, with its inner logic. In contrast, the technique of the culture industry is, from the
beginning, one of distribution and mechanical reproduction, and therefore always remains external to its
object.[43]

The distinction between the two types of technique was
especially important for Adorno in his now famous dispute with Benjamin over the latter's essay on 'The Work
of Art in the Era of Mechanical Reproduction'.[44] Whereas
Benjamin had optimistically argued that the invasion of
aesthetic production by technological reproduction had
created the possibility for a politically progressive mass
art, Adorno replied that a more genuinely emancipatory
potential existed in the internal development of artistic
technique within seemingly autonomous works of art.
'Technical development as such can serve crude reaction
as soon as it has established itself as a fetish and by its
perfection represents the neglected social tasks as already
accomplished.'[45] Because exoteric art resisted the false
assumption that such tasks were on the verge of being
accomplished, an assumption that underlay the Weimar
left's collapse of art and political practice, it was more
truly progressive than the esoteric art, like film,
championed by Benjamin, or the 'community music'
written by leftist composers like Hanns Eisler.[46]

Even when the magical aura traditionally surrounding
esoteric art was dissolved – indeed, as we will see shortly,
precisely because it underwent such a process of
de-auraticization – such art was less prone to the fetishistic, phantasmagoric abuse of the culture industry than
even the most politically correct mass art. As Adorno
wrote to Benjamin in the midst of their dispute,

Precisely the uttermost consistency in the pursuit of the
technical laws of autonomous art changes this art and
instead of rendering it into a taboo or fetish, brings it

125

close to the state of freedom, of something that can be consciously produced and made. I know of no better materialistic programme than that statement by Mallarmé in which he defined works of literature as something not inspired but made out of words.[47]

Modern technologically reproduced art like film was deficient precisely because it lacked any significant trace of individual artistic technique.

To mention film is to remind us that Adorno's critique of the culture industry was broadly based on more than just the popular music he so despised. Although he was not as visually sensitive as Kracauer, he often used examples from contemporary movies and cartoons to illustrate his arguments. In contrast to his friend, who saw film as the 'redemption of physical reality',[48] Adorno was wary of the representational fidelity of movies, with their powerful unity of sight and sound. Reducing the distance between art and the current life was the opposite of the type of redemption he sought:

> Real life is becoming indistinguishable from the movies. The sound film, far surpassing the theatre of illusion, leaves no room for imagination or reflection on the part of the audience, who is unable to respond within the structure of the film, yet deviate from its precise detail without losing the thread of the story; hence the film forces its victims to equate it directly with reality.[49]

In more general terms, Adorno also suspected the film because he saw the eye more closely adapted to the world of bourgeois rationalism than the ear, which had 'archaic'[50] residues that prevented its total absorption into the administered world. When he did hold out hope for a critical use of film, as in his collaborative effort with Eisler on *Composing for the Films*, it was largely in terms of its musical rather than visual effects.

The book's activist insistence on film's critical potential

may, of course, be attributable more to Eisler than Adorno, who refused to acknowledge his co-authorship when the book appeared. But interestingly, it was also to film that Adorno looked near the end of his life for some relief from the relentlessly suffocating effects of the culture industry. In 'Transparencies on Film',[51] an essay reflecting on the New German Cinema launched in 1966 by governmental support of radical young film-makers like Alexander Kluge and Volker Schlöndorff, Adorno reconsidered his judgment that film was solely a product of the culture industry. Although it would be mistaken to describe this piece as a totally new departure in his work – even *Dialectic of Enlightenment* admitted that 'the culture industry does retain a trace of something better in those features which bring it close to the circus'[52] – Adorno for the first time acknowledged a critical potential within the mainstream of the culture industry. 'In its attempts to manipulate the masses,' he now conceded, 'the ideology of the culture industry itself becomes as internally antagonistic as the very society which it aims to control. The ideology of the culture industry contains the antidote to its own lie.'[53] Thus, the possibility of an immanent critique based on the existence of an actual ideology was now once again possible. Technology had not entirely replaced ideology, but could be seen as a new form of it. The glacier does move after all.

Reflecting on the way in which the new films that he now respected called ideology into question, Adorno fixed on the time-honoured technique developed earlier by radical avant-garde film-makers like Eisenstein:

Film is faced with the dilemma of finding a procedure which neither lapses into arts-and-crafts nor slips into a more documentary mode. The obvious answer today, as forty years ago, is that of montage which does not interfere with things but rather arranges them in a constellation akin to that of writing.[54]

127

But he then added, drawing on the argument he had made against Benjamin and Surrealism many years before, 'The viability of a procedure based on the principle of shock, however, raises doubts. Pure montage, without the addition of intentionality in its details, refuses to accept intentions merely from the principle itself.'[55] Such intentionality must be introduced in other ways, one of which, Adorno argued, was the interaction of films with other media, most notably advanced music. It might even then be possible to turn the collective impulses of film in a critical direction, as Benjamin had originally contended. 'The liberated film would have to wrest its *a priori* collectivity from the mechanisms of unconscious and irrational influence and enlist this collectivity in the service of emancipatory intentions.'[56]

It was in a similar mood that Adorno ruminated in an essay of 1969 called 'Leisure'[57] on the limitations of the culture industry's power to manipulate mass consciousness. Discussing a study conducted by the Institute of Social Research on the German public's reaction to the wedding of the Dutch Princess Beatrix to the German Claus von Amberg, he expressed his surprise that a general scepticism survived all the media's attempts to inflate the event's importance. 'The integration of consciousness and leisure', he concluded, 'is obviously not yet entirely successful. The real interests of the individuals are still strong enough, at the margins, to resist total control.'[58]

It would, however, be an exaggeration to characterize Adorno's second thoughts as a mellowing of his hostility towards the culture industry as a whole. Perhaps the best that might be said is that it reflected a long overdue abandonment of his assumption of a tacit identity between American popular culture and its fascist counterpart. In any event, an overriding continuity in Adorno's thought was clearly expressed in his reconsideration of the film's critical potential because of its use of the old modernist technique of montage. For as all observers have noted, his counter-conception to the culture industry was not high or serious culture *per se,* but only that variant of it identified with the twentieth century's modernist avant-garde.

Here, too, however, discriminations have to be made, for Adorno was by no means a defender of all modernist currents. Indeed, in his distaste for some he gave little ground to his alleged antipode in Marxist aesthetics, Lukács, whose alternative, critical realism, he nonetheless rejected. If Adorno was hostile to the collapse of art into life as currently lived that characterized the culture industry, he was no more sympathetic to those modernisms like Surrealism or the Neue Sachlichkeit that tried to do the same. Although he recognized the cost of too rigid a separation – contact between art and society, he insisted, is 'something which the work of greatest integrity cannot do without, if it is not to perish'[59] – he nonetheless insisted that the most fruitful contact in the administered world was one which resisted the absorption of esoteric art into everyday life. For all of his opposition to Lukács's blanket condemnation of modernism, Adorno shared his distrust of those versions that seemed all too willing to mirror the reification of modern life without protest. Thus, in contrast to Benjamin, he had no use for Surrealism's anti-subjectivist use of juxtaposed images, which he saw as lifeless and static.

> The dialectical pictures of Surrealism are those of a dialectic of subjective freedom in a situation of objective unfreedom. . . . Its montages are the true still lifes. In as much as they arrange the archaic they create *nature morte.* These pictures are not so much those of an inner essence; rather they are object-fetishes on which the subjective, the libido, was once fixated. They bring back childhood by fetishism and not by self-submersion.[60]

Even when modernist movements were expressly leftist in political orientation, Adorno looked askance at their emancipatory credentials. Convinced that the overt relation between art and politics should, at least for the present, be completely severed, he defended only those modernisms that withdrew from direct political or social commitment. Against Brecht and Sartre, he argued, 'This is not the time for political art, but politics has migrated into autonomous art, and nowhere more so than where it seems to be politically dead.'[61] Only writers like Beckett, Celan or Kafka, who refused to flinch from the breakdown of communicability, were true to the critical power of art. Only they bore agonized witness to the decimation of the subject in modern life, which both the modernist didacticism of Brecht and the 'healthy' realism supported by Lukács failed to acknowledge. Only they wrested from the objective disintegration of language a negative image of a world in which meaning might one day be achieved.

If there was any one modernist movement that encapsulated Adorno's conception of a critical avant-garde, it was, as Eugene Lunn has recently demonstrated,[62] the Expressionism that was so powerful in the Germany and Austria of his youth. Although Adorno did not become as closely identified with Expressionism as Bloch, who engaged in a bitter debate with Lukács over its implications in the 1930s,[63] his model of modernism at its most progressive was the same. From his very first essay, which was devoted to the truthfulness (*Wahrhaftigkeit*) of Expressionism's destruction of received aesthetic forms,[64] he returned again and again to its importance. Although his primary emphasis was on musical versions of Expressionism, he also deeply respected such literary figures as Kafka and Trakl. Like Horkheimer, whose earliest writings were also marked by Expressionist sympathies,[65] he never abandoned the utopian, deeply ethical impulse that more sober modernisms like the Neue Sachlichkeit would lose. Nor did he relinquish his belief that Expressionism had been the modernism most sensitive to the ways in which the administered world thwarted the realization of utopia, most notably through its graphic depiction of the anguish produced by the dissolution of the bourgeois sub-ject. What made Expressionism ultimately loyal to the utopian promise of happiness in art at its best was its ruthless fidelity to the suffering of modern man, which later modernisms often failed to register.

The most painful example of that failure for Adorno came, as might be expected, in the realm of music, for it occurred within the very school in which he was trained, the 'new music' of Schoenberg, Berg and Webern. To understand Adorno's complicated reasoning, we must now turn to the daunting task of explicating his remark-able writings on music, which are scheduled to fill twelve of the projected twenty-three volumes of his collected works.

What immediately strikes the reader of any of Adorno's analyses of music is the inadequacy of simply calling him a musicologist. As in so many other areas, his work trans-cended traditional categories. Although he was fully equipped to probe the internal development of music in strictly formal terms, he never remained solely within the sphere of musical form alone. There are, in fact, few sustained analyses of entire compositions in his work,[66] which tends instead to juxtapose fragments from a com-poser's entire *oeuvre* in the way that Benjamin sifted through the ruins of traditional culture. As was also the case when he wrote on other cultural phenomena, Adorno always moved out from the music to society, albeit in the complicated ways we will discuss shortly.

It might therefore be better to classify him essentially as a sociologist of music, which was in fact a term he often used to describe his work.[67] As such, he was a worthy successor to Max Weber, whose pathbreaking *Rational and Social Foundations of Music* was published post-humously in 1921, a scant decade before Adorno's first systematic analysis, 'On the Social Situation of Music', appeared in the inaugural issues of the Institute's new *Zeitschrift*.[68] But as his critical attitude towards the empirical sociology of music of Silbermann demonstrates, his variant of that new discipline was composed in a very unconventional key.

One of the reasons for the difference was his cautious willingness to introduce psychological categories, even though he distrusted their naturalist implications and was uninterested in music's impact on the emotions of its listeners.[69] While he called *Philosophy of Modern Music* an 'extended appendix' to *Dialectic of Enlightenment*, there are many passages that sound more like a gloss on *The Authoritarian Personality*. But the major reason Adorno's musical writings are more than just sociological is their obvious indebtedness to his philosophy of negative dialectics. When Adorno spoke of the 'musical subject', all of the resonances of that term in his philosophy are present. And it was only because he held to a particular notion of substantive rationality that he could gain some distance from Weber's analysis of the rationalization of music, which was dependent on a less complicated concept of reason. It is perhaps best therefore to speak of Adorno's 'music philosophy', as the title of Lucia Sziborsky's survey of his writings in this area suggests.[70]

But here too, it is necessary to introduce a caveat, for Adorno's work on music ought not to be confused with the tradition of philosophical aesthetics that began in eighteenth-century Germany with Baumgarten and Kant and was extended to music by such nineteenth-century figures as Hegel, Schopenhauer, Hanslick and Nietzsche.[71] For Adorno took to heart Schoenberg's celebrated critique of traditional aesthetics in his *Harmonielehre* of 1911 in favour of a more modest theory of craftsmanship that would privilege no absolute aesthetic standards. It was for this reason, in fact, that Adorno was often reluctant to identify Schoenberg and his followers as a distinct 'school' with all the conformity to aesthetic canons that such a term implied.[72] His, therefore, was a philosophy of music that registered the impossiblity of a fully coherent, systematic, positive aesthetics in our time.

Not surprisingly, more modest students of the subject found Adorno's over-determined and uncategorizable analyses of music hard to appreciate. Even his teacher and friend Alban Berg found Adorno's 'philosophical ballast' a troublesome 'fad',[73] and Schoenberg himself was still more unsympathetic, especially after the unhappy incident with *Doctor Faustus*.[74] To supporters of composers he disliked, such as Stravinsky's devotee Robert Craft, the whole project of linking music with a philosophy of history and sociology was perniciously ideological, the imposition of a determinist scheme on the random course of musical development.[75]

Although it would be difficult to dispel all the suspicions of his critics that his judgments were sometimes arbitrary and his interpretations a bit too ingenious, the logic of Adorno's work on music becomes more compelling when it is placed against the backdrop of the larger argument that we have been sketching in this book. For only then can the underlying reasoning behind his often apparently apodictic pronouncements be understood.

Perhaps the best way to approach Adorno's work in this area is to focus on the delicate relationship he claimed existed between music and society:

> The relation of works of art to society is comparable to Leibniz's monad. Windowless – that is to say, without being conscious of society, and in any event without being constantly and necessarily accompanied by this consciousness – the works of art, and notably of music which is far removed from concepts, represent society. Music, one might think, does this the more deeply the less it blinks in the direction of society.[76]

Music, in other words, is a non-conceptual, non-discursive language, which unselfconsciously 're-presents' the social world outside it. That such a re-presentation can be more than a simple mirroring is what allows art at its best to transcend as well as register what is outside its windowless monadic walls.

133

At the heart of his argument was the assumption that music was an historical rather than natural phenomenon, the reworking of 'sedimented *Geist*',[77] and not just the manipulation of mathematical regularities in acoustic events. As might be expected of a defender of Schoenberg, Adorno was particularly set on refuting the notion that the traditional tonality of Western music was somehow more natural than other musical forms. Traditional tonality, he argued, represented only a particular stage in the development of music that had now been superseded by another. That music had a history which could not be arbitrarily reversed was also a premise of his argument, which he turned against all attempts to restore tonality or other outmoded forms. Musical development need not be seen as progress, but it was historically unidirectional nonetheless.

A second major premise of Adorno's position was his claim that society as a whole was present in music and not merely the consciousness of one specific group within it. Against other Marxist aestheticians like Lucien Goldmann, who wanted to establish links between classes, their world-views and specific works of art, Adorno contended that

> The search for correspondences between class membership and a composer's social origin involves an error in principle. The strongest argument against it is not even that in music the social standpoint which an individual occupies is not directly translated into tone language. To be considered first of all is whether, from the viewpoint of the producers' class membership, there has ever been anything other than bourgeois music – a problem, by the way, which affects the sociology of art far beyond music.[78]

The general indifference to the intermediate levels between individual and the social whole that we noted in his more directly sociological work was repeated here in his sociology of music. Uninterested in the specific class background of composers or their audiences, he emphasized instead the objective implications of the works themselves for revealing the contradictions of bourgeois society.

A third premise of Adorno's argument was that aesthetic merit and social content were inseparable, contrary to the belief of most other sociologists of music. As he wrote to his friend, the composer Ernst Krenek, in 1932, 'The social question can only be meaningfully posed *on the basis* of the aesthetic *quality* question. In other words, sociology should not question how music functions, but how it stands towards fundamental social antinomies, whether it sets about to master them or let them remain or even hide them, and this question leads only to what is immanent in the form of the work in itself.'[79]

Adorno's initial attempt to probe the social situation of music came in the essay he contributed to the first issues of the *Zeitschrift*, an essay far more theoretical than the myriad reviews and analyses he had written for journals like *Anbruch, Pult und Taktstock, Zeitschrift für Musik* and *Der Scheinwerfer* during the previous decade. It was also much more explicitly Marxist, so much so in fact that he shied away from including it in any of his later collections after his return to Germany. The reason he gave for distancing himself from it appeared in a footnote to his *Introduction to the Sociology of Music*, where he called the essay's error its 'flat identification of the concept of musical production with the precedence of the economic sphere of production, without considering how far that which we call production already presupposes social production and depends on it as much as it is sundered from it'.[80] This explanation suggests a loosening of the causal relation he originally posited between superstructure and socio-economic base, but it shows how adamant he was about linking art and society even when the former seemed most autonomous.

In the original essay, in fact, the causality he proposed

135

was by no means simplistically formulated. Although Adorno began by saying, 'No matter where music is heard today, it sketches in the clearest possible lines the contradictions and flaws which cut through the present-day society,' he then quickly added, 'At the same time, music is separated from this same society by the deepest of all flaws produced by this society itself.'[81] The process of alienation, differentiation and rationalization characterized by Weber as modernization and Lukács as capitalist reification meant that music was no longer intimately tied to the practices and rituals of everyday life. Its separation into a sphere all its own, the allegedly pure music celebrated by aestheticians like Hanslick, did not mean, however, that it had achieved a true liberation from the reification and alienation it seemed to leave behind. First, Adorno argued, most music had in fact become a kind of commodity produced only for sale in the market place and thus was part of what he later would call the culture industry. And second, even when some music was able to resist this fate, its content had to reflect the sorry situation which produced the split between art and life, a split which 'cannot be corrected within music, but only within society'.[82]

That some music could transcend rather than merely reflect the existing society Adorno did not doubt, but it could do so only by refusing to paper over its contradictions:

> Music will be better, the more deeply it is able to express – in the antinomies of its own formal language – the exigency of the social situation and to call for change through the coded language of suffering. It is not for music to stare in helpless horror at society. It fulfils its social function more precisely when it presents social problems through its own material and according to its own formal laws – problems which music contains within itself in the innermost cells of its technique.[83]

136

This task likened music to critical social theory, Adorno went on, because both could negate the status quo. It was also like theory because of its resistance to the empirical consciousness of the average listener.

In 1932, Adorno was not quite ready to split critical theory or critical music entirely from its practical impact. Like theory, he wrote, 'Music which has achieved self-consciousness of its social function will enter into a dialectical relation to praxis.'[84] Whereas the well-meaning, but ultimately impotent '*Gebrauchsmusik*' (use music) of a Hindemith or the '*Gemeinschaftsmusik*' (community music) of an Eisler attempted to achieve this relation through an immediate impact on their audience, only a music that refuses easy communicability can be said to be truly revolutionary.

> Within present society, such music encounters a vehement resistance which surpasses the resistance against all use music and communal music, no matter how literary or political its accents might be. Nonetheless, this resistance seems to indicate that the dialectical function of this music is already perceptible in praxis, even if only as a negative force, i.e., as 'destruction'.[85]

To understand why Adorno felt only a certain version of this inaccessible 'destructive' music was truly critical, we must examine more closely his general argument about music's relation to society. Through complicated dialectical analyses of the production, reproduction and consumption of music, Adorno explored virtually all facets of that relation. The most important of these, however, was production, for 'the social distribution and reception of music is a mere epiphenomenon; the essence is the objective social constitution of music itself'.[86] By the production of music he meant the process of composition, which he wanted to rescue from the equally fallacious notions that it represented the composer's sovereign genius or his total domination by external forces. All genuine music, he contended, is a 'force-field of constructive and mimetic moments and no more exhausted in either kind than any other such field'.[87] The true 'musical subject' is thus 'not individual, but collective',[88] a composite of the composer's personal skills and the means at his disposal bequeathed by the past. Musical production was thus neither entirely autonomous, nor reducible to the social production it partly reflected. Composing, as he told the somewhat sceptical Krenek, 'is a type of deciphering (or also of self-remembering); the "text" is looked at long enough until it illuminates itself and that sudden flash of illumination, the spark in which the "meaning" lies, is the productive moment. . . . I don't want to deny the subjective side of the dialectic, but only its "autarky", which is precisely what dialectics must sublate, and that is why the dialectical materialist concept is so important for me.'[89]

Because composition is a kind of decoding, it is not reducible to its constructive moment, the objectification of the composer's subjectivity, but rather contains a necessary moment of mimesis as well. The central role of mimesis in Adorno's general aesthetic theory will be made clearer shortly, but in musical terms, it meant *inter alia* that pure sounds were also expressions of an external social reality. 'Musical material', as he liked to call the tone combinations, at once form and content, available to any composer at a particular time, was related to the material reality of society. The rationalization of the latter also had its indirect effect on the rationalization of the former. Although, as we have seen, Adorno wanted to distinguish artistic productive technique from technology in the larger sense, he was sensitive to the ways in which the two might be related.

Beyond the production of music was its reproduction, a distinction that followed from the division of labour between composer and performer, score and instrumental realization, concert event and technical transmission or preservation. With remarkable learning, Adorno explored all facets of reproduction, the various mediations between producer and consumer in the bourgeois era. Whether it be the relation of chamber music to the private space of the bourgeois home, the sinister link between flamboyant, dominating conductors and the *Führerprinzip* of fascism, or the impact of radio broadcasts on the destruction of the music's aura, Adorno had provocative and original comments to make on the implications of reproduction in the musical life of the West. That he valued the very distinction between production and reproduction as an emblem of the non-identity between music's abstract essence and sensuous appearance, the composer's thought and the musician's interpretation, is demonstrated by his uneasiness with the virtual collapse of the distinction in the electronic music of the mid-twentieth century. The de-differentiation implied by such a collapse marked the increased integration of musical negation into the administered world. 'Technological development, understood at first as extra-musical, then guarded by compositional intentions, converges with inner-musical development. If works of art become their own reproduction, it is then foreseeable that reproductions will become works.'[90] The result comes perilously close to that process of instrumentalizing art which occurs in the culture industry: 'The tension between technique and content is necessarily reduced further. The less musical portrayal continues to be the portrayal of something, the more the essence of the means comes to agree with the essence of that which is portrayed.'[91]

Finally, Adorno also investigated the reception of music, although with far more scepticism than empirically minded sociologists of music. From his dissection of the 'regression of hearing' in his 1938 essay in the *Zeitschrift* to his typology of listeners in his 1962 *Introduction to the Sociology of Music*,[92] Adorno lamented the decline of the capacity to respond critically and knowledgeably to music, a decline which paralleled the increasing power of the culture industry. Although it is easy to detect the contempt of the arrogant expert in his remarks, Adorno insisted that

> the prevailing condition envisioned by critical typology is not the fault of those who listen one way rather than another. It is not even the fault of the system, of the culture industry that buttresses the state of mind of people so as to be better able to exploit it. Instead, the condition arises from the nethermost sociological layers: from the separation of mental and manual labour, or of high and low forms of art; later from the socialized semi-culture; ultimately from the fact that the right consciousness in the wrong world is impossible, and that even the modes of social reaction to music are in thrall to the false consciousness.[93]

Adorno's sensitivity to the ambiguities and contradictions implicit in whatever type of listening or criticism he might defend also informed his extensive writing on the immanent development of musical language itself. There was no composer, not even Schoenberg, who escaped the aporias of culture produced by the dialectic of enlightenment. That dialectic began for Adorno in musical terms essentially with the work of Bach, whose modernity he defended in an essay directed against recent attempts to interpret his music as an expression of archaic Being.[94] Endorsing Schoenberg's view of Bach, Adorno claimed that it was he who first introduced the 'technique of the developing variation, which then became the basic compositional technique in Viennese Classicism'.[95] The social source of the breakthrough, he speculated, was the transformation of craft production into manufacturing, which meant the rationalization of the production process through its decomposition into smaller elements. 'If this resulted in the rationalization of material production, then Bach was the first to crystallize the idea of the rationally constituted work, of the aesthetic domination of nature.'[96] The culmination of the musical domination of nature

140

begun by Bach occurred, according to Adorno, in the twentieth century. The highpoint of the technique of developing variation he would place much earlier in the work of Beethoven, specifically in his so-called middle period (normally seen as beginning with the *Third Symphony* in 1803 or 1804 and extending to about 1819 with his piano sonata, Opus 106). Although Adorno never finished the philosophical investigation of Beethoven he began in the 1930s – the manuscript is scheduled for publication as Volume 21 of the Collected Works – it has been obvious to all commentators that he was the composer who represented Adorno's model of greatest musical achievement, the touchstone of all his judgments on later figures.[97]

It has long been a staple of musical criticism to link Beethoven with the heroic age of high bourgeois culture, the revolutionary era out of which German Idealism and dialectical thought also emerged. Such works as the *Eroica*, *Fidelio* and the *Ninth Symphony* can easily be seen as expressions of the bourgeoisie's rising self-confidence as the putative universal class representing mankind. Although students of his work often disagree over Beethoven's precise relation to the extra-musical events of the period or fight over his being closer to Kant or Hegel,[98] the remarkable mediation of classical (or Enlightenment) and romantic elements in his music has made him appear to be the typification of bourgeois culture in its hour of greatest triumph.

Adorno was in part attracted to Beethoven for this very reason. As the culmination of the secularizing process that freed music from its religious entanglement, a process that Adorno saw beginning with Bach, Beethoven represented the highest moment of bourgeois humanism, the clearest embodiment of practical reason in sensuous terms, the greatest realization of active subjectivity in objective musical material. No longer dependent on pleasing aristocratic patrons in the manner of Mozart and Haydn, Beethoven was at one with the new audience created by the emancipation of the bourgeoisie, an audience that could appreciate the beauty of his music and identify with its truth. In the sonata form, which Beethoven brought to perfection in his symphonies and string quartets, the ancient ideal of the art work as an organic whole was actually realized.

> The kinship with that bourgeois libertarianism which rings all through Beethoven's music is a kinship of the dynamically unfolding totality. It is in fitting together under their own law, as becoming, negating, confirming themselves and the whole without looking outward, that his movements come to resemble the world whose forces move them; they do not do it by imitating that world.[99]

The crucial phrase here is 'dynamically unfolding totality', which expressed Adorno's appreciation for the progressively temporal dimension of music and for the possibility of achieving totality through the masterful uses of reprises that were like the dialectical reconciliations in Hegel's *Phenomenology*. Insofar as Adorno was hostile to affirmative uses of totality in the ways we have examined in previous chapters, it may seem surprising to see him so unequivocally favourable in regard to music. There was, however, a crucial difference for him between totality in theoretical terms and in musical ones. Whereas the former is essentially conceptual and thus threatens to dominate the non-identical and heterogeneous particulars subsumed under it, the latter is non-conceptual and thus less inclined to eliminate otherness. The irreducibly mimetic moment in music means it can never be wholly a construction of the dominating subject, as can both idealist and positivist philosophies. In this sense, Beethoven was closer to a utopian materialist holism than the great philosophers of his day with their hostility to the 'preponderance of the object'.

In one respect, however, Beethoven shared a weakness

with his philosophical contemporaries, for like their totalizations, his too had an inevitably ideological dimension. The bourgeoisie, after all, was not a genuinely universal class. Like the Jacobins in the French Revolution or Kant with his assertion of a freedom that had to be there in all men, there was a forced quality to Beethoven's celebration of emancipation:

> That the affirmative gestures of the reprise in some of Beethoven's greatest symphonies assume the force of crushing repression, of an authoritarian 'That's how it is', that the decorative gestures overshoot the musical events – this is the tribute Beethoven was forced to pay to the ideological character whose spell extends even to the most sublime music ever to mean freedom by continued un-freedom.[100]

Nonetheless, if Adorno ever had a positive vision of the reconciled work of art as a prefiguration of a rationally totalized, yet non-dominating social whole, it was in the music of Beethoven's middle period.

Adorno's interest in Beethoven was not, however, restricted to his most affirmative compositions. In fact, the two published fragments of his larger project, 'Beethoven's Late Style' and 'Alienated Masterpiece: the *Missa Solemnis*',[101] were devoted to Beethoven's controversial third period, which lasted from about 1819 to his death in 1828. Rather than attributing the changes in Beethoven's style to his personal infirmities, as sometimes has been done, Adorno explained them in more general terms as a reflection of the growing crisis of the bourgeois revolution, which lost its momentum after the defeat of Napoleon. Unlike Hegel, however, Beethoven refused to reconcile himself to the new realities of Restoration Europe; the late work, with the great exception of the still affirmative *Ninth Symphony* (which, to be sure, Beethoven had planned as early as 1812), struggled against the collapse of the revolutionary synthesis.

143

Beethoven's final works, in particular the late quartets, so Adorno contended, remained both subjective and objective, but without the mediation of the two poles he had been able to achieve earlier:

> The fragmented landscape of the work is objective; the light which alone causes it to radiate is subjective. Beethoven does not bring about a harmonious synthesis of these extremes. Rather, he tears them apart, as the force of dissociation, in time, perhaps to preserve them for eternity. In the history of art, late works are catastrophes.[102]

The particular 'catastrophe' in which Adorno was interested was the *Missa Solemnis*, which was unintelligible to most of its first listeners. By returning to the seemingly archaic form of the religious mass, the composer, still himself a secular humanist, registered the failure of the bourgeois emancipation from its pre-enlightened past. By disappointing the expectations of his audience, he registered the growing alienation of the artist from his public, which deepened as the century wore on. Perhaps most significant of all, by abandoning the sonata form with its developing variation in favour of more static contrapuntal forms, he called into question the bourgeois subject's achievement of genuine autonomy. No longer a model of organic wholeness based on dialectical reconciliations, Beethoven's late music achieved whatever totalization it did by forced means:

> While the category of totality, which in Beethoven's works is always the major one, results in other works from the internal development of the individual parts, it is retained in the *Missa* only at the price of a kind of levelling. The omnipresent stylization principle no longer tolerates anything which is truly unique and whittles the character of the work down to the level of the scholastic. These motifs and themes resist being named.

The lack of dialectical contrasts which are replaced by the mere opposition of closed phrases weakens at times the totality.[103]

But what made the *Missa* so important for Adorno was less its feeble attempt to preserve some sort of totality than its willingness to call alienation by its own name. To put it in terms that Adorno borrowed from Benjamin, it began to assume the allegorical form that refused to reconstruct the ruins of a fragmented whole through symbolism. What Baudelaire was shortly to express in poetic terms with his internal critique of lyric poetry,[104] Beethoven was able to achieve in his music:

He exposed the classical as classicizing. He rejected the affirmative, that which uncritically endorsed Being in the idea of the classically symphonic. . . . At this moment he transcended the bourgeois spirit whose highest musical manifestation was his own work. Something in his own genius, the deepest part of it, refused to reconcile in a single image what is not reconciled.[105]

Subsequent attempts to reassert symbolic unity, such as those made by Schubert, resulted in a brittle structural whole, more crystalline than organic.[106]

In fact, virtually all of the nineteenth-century music after Beethoven failed to achieve either the dialectical totalizations of his second period or the allegorical detotalizations of his third. Adorno's analysis of that failure tended, as Rose Rosengard Subotnik has recently noted,[107] to homogenize the music into one essential pattern. Perhaps the major reason for the relatively undifferentiated quality of Adorno's critique was the lack of any dynamic referent outside of music to which he could turn as the source of a musical breakthrough. Unlike Lukács, who also charted the decline of bourgeois culture after its heroic era, Adorno had no faith in the emergence of its proletarian successor. Thus, although Beethoven

145

may have been the musical equivalent in certain respects of Kant or Hegel, there were no composers who paralleled Marx. The basic reason was, 'The proletariat was never permitted to constitute itself as a music subject; such a creative function was made impossible both in terms of its position within the system – where it was nothing more than an object of domination – and through the repressive factors which formed its own nature.'[108] Even in the twentieth century, when Marxist composers like Eisler tried to create a self-consciously collective music to express and stimulate the revolutionary consciousness of the working class, Adorno could scarcely conceal his scorn.[109] The only musical subject he ever took seriously was the bourgeois one whose disintegration the late Beethoven was the first to record.

What made most subsequent nineteenth-century music anathema to Adorno was precisely its inability to come to terms with that change. Like the later culture industry, it either pretended to arise from a still creative individual subject, which was carried to an extreme in Romanticism, or it sought new forms of collectivity, as in the case of Wagner's search for the regeneration of the German *Volk* through a revival of mythic community. The true decadence of bourgeois culture – and Adorno explicitly used that term, although he elsewhere attacked Lukács for employing it[110] – was most evident, in fact, in Wagner, whose significance Adorno explored in a book begun in the late 1930s and published in 1952.[111]

In Search of Wagner was deeply coloured by what Adorno saw as the link between Wagner's music, his 'social character' and the regressive forces in bourgeois society that ultimately fed fascism. Although he was always somewhat dubious about opera (with the great exception of Berg's works) because of its inferiority to imageless, pure music, and its reliance on a now decayed aura, his animus towards Wagner was clearly influenced by non-musical factors. Basing his argument on the 'anthropology' of the early bourgeois protest movements

146

sketched by Horkheimer in his 'Egoism and the Freedom Movement',[112] Adorno insisted on the essential continuity between Wagner's anti-Semitic, racist beliefs, his sado-masochistic, authoritarian personality and his music. Like Nietzsche before him and a host of others after, he refused to absolve the music from the taint of Wagner's ideas and character.

The most interesting aspect of his analysis for our purposes concerns the music itself, which typified, in quintessential form, the degeneration of bourgeois musical self-consciousness after the late Beethoven. Unlike more recent critics such as Joseph Kerman, who see Wagner as bringing the symphonic achievement of Beethoven into the opera house,[113] Adorno depicted the two composers as diametrical opposites. Whereas Beethoven's symphonies were examples of coherently totalized works in which strong subjects realized their subjectivity in objective form, Wagner's operas lacked any real principle of development or genuine subjectivity. His famous reliance on 'infinite melody' was like Hegel's 'bad infinity', an endless succession of directionless changes without any real resolution. Instead of expressing classical bourgeois man's triumphant struggle to assert himself, Wagner's operas betrayed late bourgeois man's capitulation to reified forces outside his control.

Anticipating the culture industry and the regression of hearing in the twentieth century, Wagner resorted to such techniques as the leitmotif, which corresponded to the breakdown of organic totalization in his music. Among its other purposes, Adorno wrote, can be found 'a commodity-function, rather like that of an advertisement: anticipating the universal practice of mass culture later on, the music is designed to be remembered, it is intended for the forgetful'.[114] Leitmotifs pander to the musical equivalent of the ego-weakness that will lead to authoritarian personalities in our own era.

The reverse side of Wagner's atomized, undeveloped motifs, according to Adorno, was the veneer of wholeness

147

forced on the music from without, which is given ideological justification with the concept of the *Gesamtkunstwerk*:

> In the dubious quid pro quo of gestural, expressive and structural elements on which Wagnerian form feeds, what is supposed to emerge is something like an epic totality, a rounded and complete whole of inner and outer. Wagner's music simulates this unity of the internal and external, of subject and object, instead of giving shape to the rupture between them. In this way the process of composition becomes the agent of ideology even before the latter is imported into the music dramas via literature.[115]

To cover over the still contradictory social realities he sought to resolve through musical fiat, Wagner developed the phantasmagoric techniques later so characteristic of the culture industry. The dream-like escape from real life and wilful suppression of the productive origins of the music was especially evident in Wagner's hostility to historical time in favour of mythic recurrence. 'The absence of any real harmonic progression', Adorno pointed out, 'becomes the phantasmagorical emblem for time standing still.'[116] The dynamism of a Beethoven is replaced by the spatialized temporality of a bourgeois culture no longer going in an upward direction. Wagner's gesture is essentially immutable and atemporal. Impotently repeating itself, music abandons the struggle within the temporal framework it mastered in the symphony.'[117] Abandoning any real hope for social change, the weakened bourgeois subject represented in Wagner's operas accepts cruel fate as a necessity, thus identifying with the aggressor.

For all his deep-seated hostility to Wagner, Adorno did not, however, refuse to see anything redeeming in his music. In Wagner's use of chromaticism, Adorno acknowledged, the emancipation of dissonance was prepared. Although Wagner tried to transfigure the suffering expressed in such dissonance rather than look it in the eye, as had the late Beethoven, his weakening of tonality did have a progressive function. Indeed, so Adorno concluded, 'There is not one decadent element in Wagner's work from which a productive mind could not extract the forces of the future. . . . Hence, Wagner is not only the willing prophet and diligent lackey of imperialism and late-bourgeois terrorism. He also possesses the neurotic's ability to contemplate his own decadence and to transcend it in an image that can withstand that all-consuming gaze.'[118] Here perhaps the best pieces of evidence are those remarkable passages of 'black, abrupt, jagged music'[119] in the third act of *Tristan* that unintentionally subvert his vision of transfiguration through death.

The reversal of decadence promised in Wagner could not, however, appear in the affirmative form of Beethoven's second period. When attempts were made to do so by composers Adorno admired, like Mahler, he claimed that they nonetheless contained a negative moment showing their realization of its impossibility, a kind of self-critique that prevented them from being merely ideological.[120] When similar attempts were made by composers towards whom he felt ambivalent, such as Bartok or Janacek, he explained their affirmative traits in terms of the 'extraterritoriality'[121] of composers from the periphery of Europe, where the rationalization of the administered world had not yet fully penetrated an earlier folk culture. When the attempts were made by composers he disliked, such as Sibelius, Hindemith or especially Stravinsky,[122] he attacked them as regressively anti-subjective and complicitous with the worst forms of reification.

The defenders of the composers he maligned quickly pointed out that such judgments often seemed arbitrary. Why, for example, was the Finn Sibelius any less extraterritorial than the Hungarian Bartok or the Czech Janacek? Why was Mahler any less *völkisch* than Stravinsky, whose cosmopolitanism was so evident?[123]

149

Was it, in fact, really possible to evaluate all music in terms of the same philosophical and social criteria, a question Adorno himself tacitly opened when he admitted that his friend Krenek's work was outside of his normal categories?[124]

Many of Adorno's judgments can perhaps be best explained by his particular training in the 1920s in the so-called 'new music' of the second Vienna School of Schoenberg and his followers. If any antidote to decadence could be found in the music of our century, it was to their work that Adorno turned. His essay on Schoenberg as the 'dialectical composer' significantly ends by placing his name 'in the landscape where the dream of freedom first found its conscious tone: Beethoven'.[125] He too was a master of 'developing variations'.[126]

But paradoxically, in Schoenberg's case, it was precisely because of his greatest achievement, the definitive overturning of the tonality of Beethoven and Western music as a whole, that he entered that landscape. During what Adorno liked to call the 'heroic decade' of modern music, which began with the *Georgelieder* in 1907, Schoenberg liberated music from the harmonizing tyranny of the dominant tonal triad. In so doing, he allowed dissonance, music with no concluding cadence, to emerge as an essential rather than accidental constituent of pieces as a whole.[127] Schoenberg's atonal phase was also his most expressionist because dissonance is among music's most compelling expressive vehicles.

But what was expressed by the atonal variations in Schoenberg was not the power of the sovereign subject, sometimes shrilly asserted by other Expressionists, but rather the *Angst* accompanying its breakdown. Moreover, Schoenberg's dialectic was materialist in its presentation of that terror, 'for the movement is situated within the material itself. The productive force which incites this movement involves the reality of a psychic drive – the drive, namely towards undisguised and uninhibited expression of the psyche and the unconscious *per se*.'[128] This drive, however, comes up against the objective limitations of the musical material, which cannot accommodate it. 'Schoenberg's really central achievement', Adorno contended, 'is that he, from his earliest works on . . . never behaved "expressionistically", superimposing his subjective intentions upon heterogeneous material in an authoritarian and inconsiderate matter.'[129] Instead, he allows the truth of the material, whose contradictions were covered over by Wagner and other affirmative composers, to emerge. Like the linguistic purism of Karl Kraus and the architectural severity of Adolf Loos, Schoenberg's music eschewed the falsely consoling ornamentation of previous art to lay bare a world from which human warmth had fled.

If Schoenberg's great atonal achievement was produced by the constraints of the musical material, with all its sedimented history, so too was the next stage in his development, the twelve-tone serialism to which he turned after his composing moratorium from 1918 to 1923. Adorno always felt profoundly ambivalent towards this aspect of the 'new music'. As early as 1929,[130] he pointed out the ominous implications of Schoenberg's attempt to restore order after the explosion of tonality. Whereas the work of Webern and Berg still remained true to the *Angst* of the eviscerated subject, the later Schoenberg began, despite his intentions, to identify more with the forces of domination. The guilt, to be sure, was not that of Schoenberg himself: 'These works are magnificent in their failure,'Adorno contended. 'It is not the composer who fails in the work; history, rather, denies the work in itself.'[131] For this reason, the two poles of *Philosophy of Modern Music*, Schoenberg and Stravinsky, began to converge.

Adorno felt essentially unsympathetic towards serialism because he saw it as the tyranny of method over material, a failure within artistic technique even more ominous than the culture industry's invasion of technique by technology. Although Schoenberg often insisted that he advocated

151

'twelve-tone *compositions* rather than *twelve-tone* compositions', his injunction to avoid repeating any given note until all eleven others were sounded meant the death knell of contingency. The rationalization of music described by Max Weber thus reached its apogee in the twelve-tone row, which was the musical version of the domination of nature described in *Dialectic of Enlightenment*:

> The total rationality of music is its total organization. By means of organization, liberated music seeks to reconstitute the lost totality – the lost power and the responsibly binding force of Beethoven. Music succeeds in so doing only at the price of its freedom, and thereby it fails. Beethoven reproduced the meaning of tonality out of subjective freedom. The new ordering of twelve-tone technique virtually extinguishes the subject.[132]

In short, Schoenberg, the dialectical composer, 'brings dialectics to a halt'.[133] Those who slavishly duplicate his method merely confirm the ageing of new music, the neutralization of its critical edge, the exhaustion of its ability to shock. 'What is forgotten today', Adorno lamented in the 1950s, 'is that twelve-tone technique is without significance except insofar as it serves to bind together centrifugal, recalcitrant and more or less explosive musical forces. Unless accompanied by this corollary and contradiction this technique has no justification and is a waste of time.'[134] Composers like Pierre Boulez, in their effort to 'wring the neck'[135] of subjectivity, thus repress the Expressionist anguish still bubbling beneath the surface in the early Schoenberg. They represent the twentieth century's even more troubling version of that flattening out of music's dynamic tensions which began in the nineteenth after the later Beethoven. Thomas Mann was therefore right – or at least in accord with Adorno's desperate view of the current situation – when he had Adrian Leverkühn 'take back' Beethoven's

Ninth Symphony at the end of *Doctor Faustus*, explaining that 'what human beings have fought for and stormed citadels, what the ecstatics exultantly announced – that is not to be'.[136]

It was, to be sure, not easy to locate when Adorno thought the promise of the *Ninth Symphony* might actually have been closer to realization. If there had been a missed opportunity, as *Negative Dialectics* suggested there was for the promise of dialectical philosophy, Adorno did not make its musical expression very clear. Indeed, as we have seen, he felt that the *Ninth Symphony* itself was too affirmative a work for the last years of Beethoven's career, which were epitomized instead by the 'alienated' *Missa Solemnis*. When he wrote about the later nineteenth century, it was Wagner's proto-fascist phantasmagoria that seemed to him typical rather than the heroic humanism of Verdi, whose operas have often been tied to the Italian Risorgimento at its best.[137] In the twentieth century, Schoenberg's atonal revolution represented for Adorno 'the surviving message of despair from the shipwrecked',[138] the death agony of the bourgeois subject brought to a head by the calamity of the First World War and fascism. But there was no inkling of a new alternative for Adorno, even in his most Marxist moments, in the socialist revolutions of the same era. By a certain stretch of the imagination, the Russian Stravinsky might have been seen as a prefiguration of a new collective subject instead of a regressive objectivism. But, of course, Adorno's imagination stretched in a very different direction and Stravinsky became the composer of fascism *malgré lui*. Without any of that fascination for the Russian soul which inspired the early Lukács and Bloch, Adorno saw only primitivist regression combined with sado-masochistic authoritarianism in Stravinsky's music. It would be hard to argue that his instincts were wrong when it came to the Soviet Union, but in musical terms, what might almost be called his fetishization of the dying bourgeois subject meant he was closed to any potential alternatives.

153

There were, in fact, few specific examples of music in the mid-twentieth century to which Adorno could turn for relief from his saturnine vision of music's decay. There was nothing remotely redemptive in popular music that was comparable to the new cinema he began cautiously to praise in the 1960s. Nor were serious composers, with the possible exception of John Cage with his use of Beckett-like silences, much more attractive. If artists with the critical power of a Webern or Berg were alive today, he ruminated in 1956, they would have their individualism drummed out of them by the ever-increasing powers of administration, both in the West and East.

And yet, although Adorno seems to have been unable to find any specific musical figure or trend to applaud, he nonetheless refused to relinquish his general belief that art was still the most likely repository of negation in the administered world. This strategic withdrawal into aesthetics, which can be seen as early as *Dialectic of Enlightenment* if not before, was given its most extended expression in the work Adorno was struggling to complete when overtaken by death in 1969. Remaining an unfinished torso like Benjamin's *Passagenwerk* or Schoenberg's *Oratorio*, two projects Adorno greatly admired, *Aesthetic Theory* thus provided a fittingly unresolved end to his career.

It was written during the troubled time when Adorno's quarrel with the German student movement was reaching its climax. In June 1967, he provocatively asserted his choice of aesthetics over politics through the gesture of refusing to change the topic of a lecture he planned to give on 'The Classicism of Goethe's Iphigenia' in Berlin, shortly after the killing of the student Benno Ohnesorg by the police during the visit of the Shah of Iran.[139] The strictures against committed, partisan art, which he directed against Sartre and Brecht a few years earlier, were also clearly aimed at an explicitly *engagé* aesthetic theory.

And yet, what made Adorno's retreat into aesthetics

154

still political in the deepest sense was his conviction that genuine art contained a utopian moment that pointed to a future political and social transformation. The vulgar Marxist inability to see beyond art's ideological or instrumental function was unfortunate:

> We must be especially wary of the present insufferable tendency to drag out at every slightest opportunity the concept of ideology. For ideology is untruth – false consciousness, a lie. It manifests itself in the failure of art works, in their own intrinsic falsehood, and can be uncovered by criticism. . . . The greatness of works of art lies solely in their power to let those things be heard which ideology conceals.[140]

How was that power manifest for Adorno? To do proper justice to his answer would require a close reading of the more than five hundred pages of *Aesthetic Theory*, which was written in Adorno's characteristically paratactic, anti-systematic, non-cumulative style. It would also necessitate a thorough grounding in the aesthetic theories of German Idealism, which were both a stimulus and a foil for his own position. To do so in this short compass is impossible and also, to the extent that we have already touched on many of the central themes, unnecessary. Rather than offer a paraphrase of the unparaphrasable argument of the book as a whole, it will be more useful to focus on only four of its fundamental points: the mimetic moment in art and its relation to natural beauty, the de-aestheticization of art and its relation to modernization, the idea of aesthetic experience and its relation to theory, and the truth content of art and its relation to autonomy.

The relationship between art and society posited by Adorno is, as we have seen, far more indirect and complicated than the reflection theory defended by vulgar Marxist aestheticians. Yet, for Adorno, one of the central virtues of art is its mimetic character. There are, he claimed, two implications of the term, the first suggesting

155

the imitation of the current *social* reality, the second that of the *natural* reality transformed by, but still irreducible to, the social. Adorno contended that genuine art contained both types of mimesis. As he put it in his 'Ideas on the Sociology of Music', 'Through its pure materiality, music is the art in which the pre-rational mimetic impulse asserts itself irreducibly and appears simultaneously in constellations with the march of progressive natural and material domination.'[141]

Drawing on Benjamin's notion of a mimetic faculty as the sensuous, onomatopoeic source of language,[142] Adorno contended that art expressed not only the suffering of men caused by social injustice, but also that of the nature they have so harshly dominated. The preponderance of the object he defended in philosophical terms was most clearly evident in works of art, which were irreducible to their merely constructive, subjective origins. Their mimetic moment was intrinsically utopian because it preserved a memory of man's prehistoric oneness with nature (itself perhaps recapitulated in the childhood memories of civilized man) and was thus a prefiguration of a possible restoration of that condition in the future.

Aesthetic mimesis also contained a utopian moment in its affirmation of sensuous appearance, which philosophers ever since Plato had tended to demean as inferior to ideal essences. It was because of his appreciation of this aspect of mimesis that Adorno took issue with Hegel's hierarchical relegation of art to a status beneath religion and philosophy. For all his scepticism towards Kant's emphasis on subjective taste and judgment in aesthetic matters, he was attracted to Kant's defence of natural beauty, which Hegel had seen as inferior to its artificial counterpart. For natural beauty represented man's dependence on an object not of his own creation; it was thus a paradigm of non-identity based on a tender and respectful relationship between man and nature.

Adorno, however, did not equate art with the mimesis

of nature *per se,* but with that of natural beauty, which required a human ability to respond affirmatively to form. Thus, insofar as beauty is a function of form, art is also an organized construct, the objectification of subjectivity with links to the rationalization of the social world. What he liked to call art's 'riddle-like' character was produced by its uneasy mixture of mimetic and constructive, sensuous and rational moments. But as we have seen, the techniques used in aesthetic production were not the same as the technological means on which the social forces of production were based. Although the rationalization of aesthetic technique might be related to that of society, as Adorno suggested in his critique of the twelve-tone row, it might also resist it, as he implied in his defence of atonal music and the dramas of Beckett. But both types of rationalization were furthered by what Adorno called the 'de-aestheticization of art',[143] by which he meant its progressive liberation from the mythic, cultic, ritualized context out of which it emerged, and its pursuit of internal laws of development.

Adorno's argument for the value of de-aestheticization was an implicit critique of Benjamin's alternative of either auratic art or art collapsed into everyday life; his own preference was for a third possibility, an art that exposed its productive origins and thus lost its aura, but which nonetheless resisted penetration by external productive forces. Like the Russian formalists and the later deconstructionists, Adorno valued certain types of modernist art for their destruction of the illusion of organic, totalized beauty that underlay traditional aesthetics. As he put it in the last sentence of *Philosophy of Modern Music,* 'Art would perhaps be authentic only when it had totally rid itself of the idea of authenticity – of the concept of being-so-and-not-otherwise.'[144] There was, in other words, an aesthetic jargon of authenticity that was no less pernicious than its philosophical counterpart because it tried to resurrect the aura of a beautiful illusion that modernism ruthlessly undercut. Its admission of the 'ugly', the dis-

157

sonant, into art – which began with the Romantic fascination with the grotesque – was a sign of art's increasing
ability to call itself into question.[145] Although it inevitably
remains an illusion in an unfree world, at least de-aestheticized art knows itself as such. It refuses to try to re-
enchant the disenchanted world. It can ward off the
ever-present danger that art will turn into affirmative con-
solation by providing an illusory refuge from actual mis-
ery.

It was thus to the paradoxically de-aestheticized aesthetic experience that Adorno, for all his dislike of reception
aesthetics, turned for the most likely antidote to reification. As we noted in discussing his typology of listeners,
Adorno never claimed that any one particular version of
that experience could escape the damage done to the
subject by the dialectic of enlightenment. Yet he did feel
that the experience of art, privatized as it tended to be,
was nonetheless the best bulwark against the absolute
domination of the administered world. In *Aesthetic
Theory*, he emphasized the process-like temporal character of such experiences, which are based both on memory
and anticipation rather than the repetition of the ever-
same generated by the culture industry.[146] Moreover, because a critical response to a work of art leads beyond an
immediate emotional response to its effects, genuine
aesthetic experience inevitably entails theoretical reflection. Hence while critical philosophy is inadequate without aesthetic experience, this experience needs critical
philosophy to draw out its contradictory implications. In
this sense, even the most autonomous work of art needs
something outside itself to complete it.

Only a dialectical combination of aesthetic experience
and critical philosophy – or what Adorno would have
termed a dynamic constellation – can bring out what he
called the truth content (*Wahrheitsgehalt*) of a work of art.
As he had contended ever since his study of Kierkegaard,
art was more than irrational, subjective immediacy; it had
a cognitive status as well, pointing to the truth. Truth for

Adorno was not, as we have seen, merely correspondence between propositions and an external referent in the current world, but rather a concept with normative resonances as well, referring to a future 'true' society. It is this latter meaning that appears in such assertions as, 'In the world we live in there are always things for which art is the only remedy; there is always a contradiction between *what is* and *what is true*, between arrangements for living and humanity.'[147]

The genesis of what we might call Adorno's will to truth was the experience of pain preserved in those works of modernism which came closest to Expressionist *Angst*. For as he put it in *Negative Dialectics*, 'The need to lend a voice to suffering is a condition for all truth.'[148] If there is a positive moment in aesthetic truth, it is evident only in those works that strive for the utmost autonomy from the present society, defying immediate accessibility and popular impact. By refusing to accept the unity of art and this life, they hold out hope for a future life that will imitate art at its most utopian. For only in the utter uselessness of such works, which stubbornly resist all attempts to instrumentalize them, is the present domination of instrumental reason defied. Although in the suffering they register, they reflect the current dilemma of mankind, their mere existence as aesthetic expressions of such suffering points beyond to that 'peace as a state of distinctness without domination' whose realization, despite everything, Adorno refused to call impossible.

But, to give the screw one final twist, Adorno recognized that the fetishization of autonomy could itself be an obstacle to the realization of his utopia. As he warned in one of his essays on culture:

Through the sacrifice of its possible relation to praxis, the culture concept itself becomes an instance of organization; that which is so provokingly useless in culture is transformed into tolerated negativity or even into something negatively useful – into a lubricant for the system, into something which exists for something else, into untruth, or into goods of the culture industry calculated for the consumer.[149]

There were, in other words, no risk-free positions for the Critical Theorist in this imperfect world, no ways to derive undamaged ideas from a damaged life. The measure of Adorno's remarkable integrity as a thinker, what might be called the mark of his intellectual heroism, was his refusal to flinch from this bitter truth even in the realm of aesthetics, the very realm in which his hopes for redemption were most tenaciously grounded.

Conclusion

'ungeduldig geduldig
in namen der unbelehrbaren
lehren'[1]
HANS MAGNUS ENZENSBERGER

If, as Adorno claimed, Schoenberg's atonal music unintentionally spawned the new system of the twelve-tone
row, can the same be said of Adorno's atonal philosophy?
Did his variations also cease to develop, turning as a result
into what he observed in Benjamin, a 'dialectics at a
standstill'? Several of his most sympathetic commentators
have answered these questions in a similar way. According to Susan Buck-Morss,

> The real issue is whether Adorno's attempt at a revolu-
> tion within philosophy, modelled self-consciously after
> Schoenberg, in fact succumbed to the same fate,
> whether his principle of antisystem itself became a
> system . . . when the method of negative dialectics be-
> came total, philosophy threatened to come to a
> standstill as well, and the New Left of the 1960s not
> unjustly criticized Adorno for taking Critical Theory
> into a dead end.[2]

Irving Wohlfahrt likewise remarks,

> Adorno increasingly lacked the capacity for self-inter-
> ruption. To repeat oneself is, wrote Tretjakov, to live
> off one's capital. Adorno was unable to prevent himself
> from consolidating his assets. The later philosophy

161

tends to play endless variations on the earlier, erecting its anti-systematic impulses into a closed system which, at its very laxest, becomes a symptom of its own diagnosis.[3]

And Rose Rosengard Subotnik adds,

Adorno's criticism on a large scale (again, like twelve-tone music) seems highly repetitive, in terms of both its language and its themes, and consequently static, qualities that may preserve Adorno's individuality only at the cost of sacrificing important individual differences in the music that he studies, and qualities that Adorno himself criticizes in post-Beethovenian music as antithetical to the definition of individuality.[4]

There can, in fact, be little doubt that a lengthy journey through the thicket of Adorno's prose does give the impression of passing the same landmarks with uncomfortable frequency. But if we find ourselves apparently going in circles, retracing the contours of a latent system, despite Adorno's protestations to the contrary, two reflections may spare us the fear that the trip was not worth taking. First, the repetitive ever-sameness that Adorno so disliked in the modern world could not help but permeate his own thought. As a social physiognomy, it could scarcely avoid replicating in some respects the society it both described and hoped to change. Whether or not Adorno was blind to the genuinely dynamic impulses in our society, as his activist critics always maintain, is still uncertain. But in a century when every revolution has in some sense been betrayed, when virtually all attempts at cultural subversion have been neutralized, and when the threat of a nuclear *Aufhebung* of the dialectic of enlightenment continues unchecked, it is difficult to summon the self-confidence to call his melancholy unwarranted.

But secondly and perhaps more importantly, the form in which his latent system appeared suggests that it is not

162

really completely static after all. As we have had countless opportunities to observe, Adorno stubbornly resisted choosing between flawed alternatives or positing a harmonious mediation between them. Negative ontology or historicism, transcendent or immanent critique, autonomous art or art in the service of the revolution, speculative theory or empirical investigation – these and other antinomies Adorno held on to without forcing their reconciliation. And as we argued in our opening remarks, Adorno himself is best understood as occupying the nodal point of a dynamic force-field of tensely untotalized energies representing many of the most creative intellectual currents of our age. Much of the still explosive power of his thought derives from the complicated ways in which these elements fuse and burst asunder.

One of Adorno's favourite metaphors was, in fact, that of the torn halves of a freedom which do not add up to a whole – he used it not only in his letter of 18 March 1936 to Benjamin, but also in the first essay he contributed to the *Zeitschrift*[5] – and it is perhaps a fitting emblem of his own intellectual achievement. As such, it may suggest that Adorno was an ambitious failure, at least from the perspective of those who want solid and unequivocal answers to the questions they pose. But I think it is only fair to extend to Adorno the same exculpation that he offered to Schoenberg: 'It is not the composer who fails in the work; history, rather, denies the work in itself.' It was impossible, given that history, for Adorno to find a way out; whether or not those of us who retrieve his bottles tossed into the sea will have better luck remains very much to be seen.

Notes

Introduction

1. 'Only those thoughts are true which fail to understand themselves.' Adorno, *Minima Moralia.*
2. Adorno, *Prisms: Cultural Criticism and Society*, trans. Samuel and Shierry Weber (London, 1967), p. 150.
3. Adorno, *Minima Moralia: Reflections from Damaged Life*, trans. E. F. N. Jephcott (London, 1974), p. 50. The reference is to the Gospel of St Matthew, 7:3.
4. Adorno, *The Jargon of Authenticity*, trans. Knut Tarnowski and Frederic Will (London, 1973), p. 93.
5. Adorno, 'Auf die Frage: Was ist Deutsch', *Gesammelte Schriften*, X, 2 (Frankfurt, 1977), p. 698. *Philosophy of Modern Music* was finally translated in 1973. All titles will be given in English in the text, although not all have yet been translated. I have used the translations whenever possible, but have checked them against the original.
6. Ibid., p. 699.
7. Popper, 'Reason or Revolution?', in Adorno *et al.*, *The Positivist Dispute in German Sociology*, trans. Glyn Adey and David Frisby (London, 1976), p. 296.
8. Written by Samuel Weber for the translation of *Prisms*. It should be mentioned that several earlier essays and portions of books had been written by Adorno himself in English.
9. In addition to those mentioned in the notes above, Adorno's major translators have included E. B. Ashton, John Cumming, Anne G. Mitchell, Wesley Blomster, Willis Domingo and Rodney Livingstone. Only Ashton has translated two books, *Negative Dialectics* and *Introduction to the Sociology of Music*.
10. When Lukács quoted Adorno against himself, the latter responded: 'I do not begrudge him this: "Only those thoughts are true which fail to understand themselves", and no author can lay claim to proprietary rights over them.' But then he added, 'Nevertheless, it will need a better

argument than Lukács's to take these rights away from me.'
('Reconciliation under Duress', in *New Left Review*, ed., *Aesthetics and Politics: Debates between Bloch, Lukács, Brecht, Benjamin, Adorno*, afterword by Fredric Jameson [London, 1977], p. 167.)

11. Adorno, 'Erpresste Versöhnung', *Noten zur Literatur, Gesammelte Schriften*, XI (Frankfurt, 1974); in English, 'Reconciliation under Duress'.
12. The best discussion of Adorno's style can be found in Gillian Rose, *The Melancholy Science: an Introduction to the Thought of Theodor W. Adorno* (New York, 1978), chap. II.
13. Adorno, *Minima Moralia*, p. 86.
14. For an excellent discussion of the importance of Beckett for Adorno, see W. Martin Lüdke, *Anmerkungen zu einer 'Logik des Zerfalls': Adorno-Beckett* (Frankfurt, 1981).
15. Fritz Ringer, *The Decline of the German Mandarins: the German Academic Community, 1890–1933* (Cambridge, Mass., 1969).
16. Adorno, 'Spengler after the Decline', *Prisms*. For an interpretation that recognizes, but severely exaggerates, Adorno's debt to Spengler, see George Friedman, *The Political Philosophy of the Frankfurt School* (Ithaca and London, 1981).
17. Lukács, 1962 Preface to *The Theory of the Novel*, trans. Anna Bostock (Cambridge, Mass., 1971), p. 22.
18. Löwy, *Georg Lukács: from Romanticism to Bolshevism*, trans. Patrick Camiller (London, 1979).
19. Adorno, *Minima Moralia*, p. 192.
20. Adorno, *Prisms*, p. 26.
21. Adorno, 'Was bedeutet: Aufarbeitung der Vergangenheit', and 'Erziehung nach Auschwitz', in *Gesammelte Schriften*, X, 2.
22. Adorno, *Prisms*, p. 34.
23. Adorno, *Negative Dialectics*, trans. E. B. Ashton (New York, 1973), p. 363.
24. Adorno, *Minima Moralia*, p. 247.
25. For a discussion of the possible influence, see Susan Buck-Morss, *The Origin of Negative Dialectics: Theodor W. Adorno, Walter Benjamin, and the Frankfurt Institute* (New York, 1977), p. 5.
26. Adorno, *Negative Dialectics*, p. 362.
27. It was in that year that Jacques Derrida published *L'Écriture et la Différence*, *La Voix et la Phénomène* and *De la Grammatologie*.

28. Terry Eagleton, *Walter Benjamin or Towards a Revolutionary Criticism* (London, 1981), p. 141. For another analysis of the similarities, see Michael Ryan, *Marxism and Deconstruction: a Critical Articulation* (Baltimore, 1982), pp. 73–80.

29. See the documents in Denis Hollier, ed., *Le Collège de Sociologie (1937–1939)* (Paris, 1979). Another, even more tenuous link between Adorno and Derrida might be found through the figure of Rosenzweig, whose French disciple Emmanuel Levinas was of considerable importance for Derrida. See the latter's essay on Levinas in *Writing and Difference,* trans. with intro. Alan Bass (Chicago, 1978), which contains the very Adornoesque hypothesis that one might call the 'experience of the infinitely other, Judaism' (p. 152).

30. Derrida, 'Ein Porträt Benjamins', in *Links hatte noch alles sich zu enträtseln . . .' Walter Benjamin im Kontext,* ed. Burkhardt Lindner (Frankfurt, 1978). For an even more direct appropriation of Adorno himself by a post-structuralist, see Jean-François Lyotard, 'Adorno as the Devil', *Telos,* 19 (Spring, 1974).

31. For discussions of Adorno and Nietzsche, see Peter Pütz, 'Nietzsche and Critical Theory', *Telos,* 50 (Winter, 1981–2), and Norbert W. Bolz, 'Nietzsches Spur in der Ästhetischen Theorie', in Burkhardt Lindner and W. Martin Lüdke, eds., *Materialien zur ästhetischen Theorie Th. W. Adornos Konstruktion der Moderne* (Frankfurt, 1980).

32. Adorno, *Negative Dialectics,* p. 381.

33. Adorno, *Minima Moralia,* p. 15.

34. Author's conversation with Foucault, Berkeley, 27 October 1980.

1. A Damaged Life

1. 'Life does not live.' Quoted by Adorno, *Minima Moralia.*

2. Adorno, 'Trying to Understand *Endgame', New German Critique,* 26 (Spring/Summer, 1982), p. 126.

3. For an account of their relationship, see Martin Jay, 'Adorno and Kracauer: Notes on a Troubled Friendship', *Salmagundi,* 40 (Winter, 1978).

4. T. Wiesengrund, 'Expressionismus und künstlerische Wahrhaftigkeit: Zur Kritik neuer Dichtung', *Die Neue*

Schaubühne, 2, 9 (1920); '"Die Hochzeit des Faun":
Grundsätzliche Bemerkungen zu Bernhard Sekles' neuer
Oper', *Neue Blätter für Kunst und Literatur,* 4 and 5
(1921–2).

5. 'Die Transzendenz des Dinglichen und Noematischen in
   Husserls Phañomenologie', dissertation, University of
   Frankfurt, 1924, first published in Adorno, *Gesammelte
   Schriften,* I (Frankfurt, 1973).

6. Horkheimer, *Aus der Pubertät: Novellen und Tagebuchblätter* (Munich, 1974).

7. 'Der dialektische Komponist', in *Arnold Schönberg zum
   60. Geburtstag, 13 September 1934* (Vienna, 1934); reprinted in Adorno, *Impromptus* (Frankfurt, 1968).

8. Krenek, Preface to Theodor W. Adorno and Ernst
   Krenek, *Briefwechsel* (Frankfurt, 1974), p. 8.

9. For an account of his compositions, see René Leibowitz,
   'Der Komponist Theodor W. Adorno', in *Zeugnisse:
   Theodor W. Adorno zum sechzigsten Geburtstag*
   (Frankfurt, 1963). Among the most notable of his efforts
   was an unfinished opera based on *Tom Sawyer: Der Schatz
   des Indianer-Joe,* ed. Rolf Tiedemann (Frankfurt, 1979).

10. 'Zur gesellschaftlichen Lage der Musik', *Zeitschrift für
    Sozialforschung,* I, 1/2 and I, 3 (1932); trans. in *Telos,* 35
    (Spring, 1978).

11. 'Der Begriff des Unbewussten in der transzendentalen
    Seelenlehre', first published in *Gesammelte Schriften,* I.

12. *Kierkegaard: Konstruktion des Ästhetischen* (Frankfurt,
    1962).

13. 'The Actuality of Philosophy', *Telos,* 31 (Spring, 1977). Its
    first publication came in the initial volume of his *Gesam-
    melte Schriften* in 1973.

14. 'Die Idee der Naturgeschichte', *Gesammelte Schriften,* I.

15. *Zur Metakritik der Erkenntnistheorie: Studien über Husserl
    und phänomenologischen Antinomien* (Frankfurt, 1956), in
    translation as *Against Epistemology: a Metacritique,* trans.
    Willis Domingo (Cambridge, Mass., 1983). The best recon-
    struction of Adorno's Oxford period can be found in Carlo
    Pettazzi, *Th. Wiesengrund Adorno: Linee di origine e di
    sviluppo del pensiero (1903–1949)* (Florence, 1979), chap.
    VI.

16. Habermas, *Theorie des kommunikativen Handelns*
    (Frankfurt, 1981), vol. II, chap. VI.

17. 'Über Jazz', *Zeitschrift für Sozialforschung,* V, 3 (1936),
    under pseud. Hektor Rottweiler; 'Über den Fetischcharak-

ter in der Musik und die Regression des Hörens',
Zeitschrift für Sozialforschung, VII, 3 (1938), trans. in *The Essential Frankfurt School Reader,* eds. Andrew Arato and Eike Gebhardt, intro. Paul Piccone (New York, 1978).

18. The notes for the project were recently published by the Suhrkamp Verlag as Walter Benjamin, *Die Passagenwerk, Gesammelte Schriften,* V (Frankfurt, 1982).
19. The central letters are available in *New Left Review,* ed., *Aesthetics and Politics: Debates between Bloch, Lukács, Brecht, Benjamin, Adorno,* afterword by Fredric Jameson (London, 1977).
20. In Benjamin, *Illuminations: Essays and Reflections,* trans. Harry Zohn, ed. with intro. Hannah Arendt (New York, 1968).
21. Elizabeth Young-Bruehl, *Hannah Arendt: the Love of the World* (New Haven, 1982), p. 109.
22. Author's conversation with Pollock, Montangola, Switzerland, March 1969. In a letter to the author dated 27 January 1970, Adorno's widow Gretel affirmed that the name change was not made until 1938.
23. See the two contrasting accounts of the experience in Paul F. Lazarsfeld, 'An Episode in the History of Social Research: a Memoir', and Adorno, 'Scientific Experiences of a European Scholar in America', both in Donald Fleming and Bernard Bailyn, eds., *The Intellectual Migration: Europe and America, 1930–1960* (Cambridge, Mass., 1969).
24. 'On Popular Music', with the assistance of George Simpson, *Studies in Philosophy and Social Science,* IX, 1 (1941); 'The Radio Symphony: an Experiment in Theory', in Paul F. Lazarsfeld and Frank Stanton, eds., *Radio Research* (New York, 1941); 'A Social Critique of Radio Music', *Kenyon Review,* VII, 2 (Spring, 1945); 'Die gewürdigte Musik', in *Der getreue Korrepetitor: Lehrschriften zur musikalischen Praxis* (Frankfurt, 1963).
25. 'Fragmente über Wagner', *Zeitschrift für Sozialforschung,* VIII, 1/2 (1939); 'On Kierkegaard's Doctrine of Love', *Studies in Philosophy and Social Science,* VIII, 3 (1939); 'Spengler Today', *Studies in Philosophy and Social Science,* IX, 2 (1941); 'Veblen's Attack on Culture', *Studies in Philosophy and Social Science,* IX, 3 (1941).
26. Horkheimer, 'Egoismus und Freiheitsbewegung', *Zeitschrift für Sozialforschung,* V, 2 (1936); trans. in *Telos,* 54 (Winter, 1982–3).

27. The collection was entitled 'Walter Benjamin zum Gedächtnis' and included Horkheimer's 'Autoritärer Staat' and 'Vernunft und Selbsterhaltung', as well as Adorno's 'George und Hofmannsthal'. Benjamin's Theses are available in English in *Illuminations*.

28. Benjamin, *Illuminations*, p. 258. The same sentence appeared in his 1937 essay in the *Zeitschrift* on 'Eduard Fuchs: Collector and Historian'.

29. Benjamin, 'Linke Melancholie', *Die Gesellschaft*, VIII (1931). His target was left liberal writers like Kurt Tucholsky, Erich Kästner and Walter Mehring.

30. Pollock, 'State Capitalism: Its Possibilities and Limitations', *Studies in Philosophy and Social Science*, IX, 2 (1941); 'Is National Socialism a New Order?', *Studies in Philosophy and Social Science*, IX, 3 (1941).

31. Horkheimer, *Eclipse of Reason* (New York, 1947).

32. Horkheimer and Adorno, *Dialectic of Enlightenment*, trans. John Cumming (New York, 1972), p. 230. The translation has been modified, 'reification' replacing Cumming's mistaken 'objectification' to render '*Verdinglichung*'.

33. For a discussion of the Institute's work on anti-Semitism, see Martin Jay, 'The Jews and the Frankfurt School: Critical Theory's Analysis of Anti-Semitism', *New German Critique*, 19 (Winter, 1980). The 'Research Project on Anti-Semitism', outlined in the *Studies in Philosophy and Social Science*, IX, 1 (1941), is the first evidence of the Institute's shift.

34. Adorno, Else-Frenkel Brunswik, Daniel J. Levinson and R. Nevitt Sanford, *The Authoritarian Personality* (New York, 1950); the other volumes in the series were Nathan W. Ackerman and Marie Jahoda, *Anti-Semitism and Emotional Disorder: a Psychoanalytic Interpretation* (New York, 1950); Bruno Bettelheim and Morris Janowitz, *Dynamics of Prejudice: a Psychological and Sociological Study of Veterans* (New York, 1949); Paul Massing, *Rehearsal for Destruction* (New York, 1949); and Leo Lowenthal and Norbert Guterman, *Prophets of Deceit* (New York, 1949).

35. *Philosophy of Modern Music*, trans. Anne G. Mitchell and Wesley Blomster (New York, 1973); Hanns Eisler (and, without his name attached, Adorno), *Composing for the Films* (New York, 1947); *Minima Moralia: Reflections from Damaged Life*, trans. E. F. N. Jephcott (London, 1974).

36. Craft, 'A Bell for Adorno', *Prejudices in Disguise* (New York, 1974).

37. Mann, *The Story of a Novel: the Genesis of Doctor Faustus*, trans. Richard and Clara Winston (New York, 1961).
38. *Minima Moralia*, p. 33.
39. Ibid., p. 50.
40. Ibid., p. 211.
41. Ibid., p. 126.
42. 'Freudian Theory and the Pattern of Fascist Propaganda', in *The Essential Frankfurt School Reader*, p. 137.
43. See, for example, the essays in Johannes Heinrich von Heiseler, ed., *Die 'Frankfurter Schule' im Lichte des Marxismus* (Frankfurt, 1970).
44. 'Television and the Patterns of Mass Culture', *Quarterly of Film, Radio and Television*, VII (1954); 'The Stars Down to Earth: the *Los Angeles Times* Astrology Column', *Jahrbuch für Amerikastudien*, 2 (1957) and *Telos*, 19 (Spring, 1974); 'Prolog zum Fernsehen' and 'Fernsehen als Ideologie', *Eingriffe: Neun Kritische Modelle* (Frankfurt, 1963).
45. 'Zur gegenwärtigen Stellung der empirischen Sozialforschung in Deutschland', in *Empirische Sozialforschung*, *Schriftenreihe des Instituts zur Förderung Öffentlichen Angelegenheiten e.V.*, XVII (Frankfurt, 1952).
46. 'Was bedeutet: Aufarbeitung der Vergangenheit', *Eingriffe*, and 'Erziehung nach Auschwitz', *Stichworte: Kritische Modelle 2* (Frankfurt, 1969); both in *Gesammelte Schriften*, X, 2.
47. For an account of the estrangement from Fromm, see Martin Jay, *The Dialectical Imagination: a History of the Frankfurt School and the Institute of Social Research, 1923–1950* (Boston, 1973), chap. III.
48. Alexander and Margarete Mitscherlich, *Die Unfähigkeit zu trauern* (Munich, 1967).
49. Habermas, 'Psychic Thermidor and the Rebirth of Rebellious Subjectivity', *Berkeley Journal of Sociology*, XXV (1980), p. 2.
50. Neumann, *Behemoth: the Structure and Practice of National Socialism, 1933–1944* (New York, 1944). A German translation was finally published in 1976.
51. *Soziologische Exkurse* (Frankfurt, 1956), trans. as *Aspects of Sociology*, trans. John Viertel (Boston, 1972).
52. Letter from Horkheimer to Lowenthal, 13 April 1951, in the Lowenthal collection, Berkeley, Calif.
53. Habermas, 'The Inimitable *Zeitschrift für Sozialforschung*: How Horkheimer Took Advantage of a Historically Oppressive Hour', *Telos*, 45 (Fall, 1980), p. 116.

Notes

54. Horkheimer, Preface to *Critical Theory: Selected Essays*, trans. Matthew J. O'Connell *et al.* (New York, 1972), p. v.
55. Horkheimer, 'Die Juden und Europe', *Zeitschrift für Sozialforschung*, VIII, 1/2 (1939), p. 115.
56. On 27 January 1957, he wrote to Lowenthal, 'I believe 90 percent of all that I have published in Germany was written in America.' (Lowenthal collection.)
57. *In Search of Wagner*, trans. Rodney Livingstone (London, 1981), p. 9.
58. *Prisms: Cultural Criticism and Society*, trans. Samuel and Shierry Weber (London, 1967).
59. See, in particular, Marcuse, 'On Affirmative Culture', *Negations: Essays in Critical Theory*, trans. Jeremy J. Shapiro (Boston, 1968).
60. *Prisms*, pp. 28–9.
61. Ibid., p. 34.
62. Benjamin, *Schriften*, ed. Adorno and Gretel Adorno, 2 vols. (Frankfurt, 1955). In 1966, he and Gershom Scholem brought out an edition of Benjamin's letters. For all of his writings on Benjamin, see Adorno, *Über Walter Benjamin* (Frankfurt, 1970).
63. *Dissonanzen: Musik in der verwalteten Welt* (Göttingen, 1956); *Noten zur Literatur I* (Berlin and Frankfurt, 1958).
64. *Klangfiguren: Musikalische Schriften I* (Berlin and Frankfurt, 1959); *Mahler: Eine Musikalische Physiognomik* (Frankfurt, 1960); *Noten zur Literatur II* (Frankfurt, 1961); *Einleitung in die Musiksoziologie: Zwölf theoretische Vorlesungen* (Frankfurt, 1962), English trans. by E. B. Ashton (New York, 1976); *Eingriffe: Neun Kritische Modelle* (Frankfurt, 1963); *Der getreue Korrepetitor: Lehrschriften zur musikalischen Praxis* (Frankfurt, 1963); *Quasi una Fantasia: Musikalische Schriften II* (Frankfurt, 1963); *Moments Musicaux: Neu gedruckte Aufsätze 1928 bis 1962* (Frankfurt, 1964); *Noten zur Literatur III* (Frankfurt, 1965); *Ohne Leitbild: Parva Aesthetica* (Frankfurt, 1967); *Berg. Der Meister des kleinsten Übergangs* (Vienna, 1968); *Impromptus: Zweite Folge neu gedruckter musikalischer Aufsätze* (Frankfurt, 1968); *Stichworte: Kritische Modelle 2* (Frankfurt, 1969); *Nervenpunkte der neuen Musik* (Hamburg, 1969).
65. 'Gesellschaft', *Gesammelte Schriften*, VIII (Frankfurt, 1972), p. 15. The English version by Fredric Jameson mistranslated *Klassengesellschaft* as 'class struggle', when Adorno's point was that struggle had ended, but classes

171

remained. See 'Society', *Salmagundi*, 10–11 (Fall, 1969–Winter, 1970), p. 149.

66. 'Sociology and Empirical Research', in Adorno *et al.*, *The Positivist Dispute in German Sociology*, trans. Glyn Adey and David Frisby (London, 1976).

67. 'Sociology and Psychology', *New Left Review*, 46 (November–December 1967) and 47 (January–February 1968). The article first appeared in a *Festschrift* for Horkheimer's sixtieth birthday in 1955.

68. For a discussion of Adorno's concept of interdisciplinary research, see Martin Jay, 'Positive and Negative Totalities: Implicit Tensions in Critical Theory's Vision of Interdisciplinary Research', *Thesis Eleven*, 3 (1982).

69. See note 66.

70. Otto Stammer, ed., *Max Weber and Sociology Today*, trans. Kathleen Morris (New York, 1971).

71. *The Positivist Dispute in German Sociology*, p. 27.

72. *The Jargon of Authenticity*, trans. Knut Tarnowski and Frederic Will (London, 1973).

73. Ibid., p. 138.

74. 'Lyric Poetry and Society', *Telos*, 20 (Summer, 1974); original in *Noten zur Literatur I*.

75. *Negative Dialectics*, trans. E. B. Ashton (New York, 1973), p. 3.

76. Kolakowski, *Main Currents of Marxism*, vol. III: *The Breakdown*, trans. P. S. Falla (Oxford, 1978), p. 366.

77. *Negative Dialectics*, pp. 404–5. Translation corrected.

78. Horkheimer, *Die Sehnsucht nach dem ganz Anderen* (Hamburg, 1970).

79. 'Resignation', *Telos*, 35 (Spring, 1978), p. 168. Translation corrected.

80. Habermas, 'Consciousness-Raising or Redemptive Criticism: the Contemporaneity of Walter Benjamin', *New German Critique*, 17 (Spring, 1979), p. 43.

81. Quoted in *Die Süddeutsche Zeitung* (26–27 April 1969), p. 10.

2. Atonal Philosophy

1. 'Systems are for small people. The great ones have intuition: they wager on numbers that occur to them. . . . Their intuitions are more reliable than the laborious calculations

of the poor, which always fail because they cannot be thoroughly tested.' Heinrich Regius (Max Horkheimer), *Dämmerung.*

2. Leszek Kolakowski, *Main Currents of Marxism*, vol. I: *The Founders*, trans. P. S. Falla (Oxford, 1978), p. 1.

3. Adorno, 'Der Essay als Form', *Noten zur Literatur I* (Frankfurt, 1958). For a good discussion of its importance, see Gillian Rose, *The Melancholy Science: an Introduction to the Thought of Theodor W. Adorno* (New York, 1978), p. 14f. It is reprinted in volume II of the *Gesammelte Schriften.*

4. Adorno, *Stichworte: Kritische Modelle 2* (Frankfurt, 1969); *The Essential Frankfurt School Reader,* eds. Andrew Arato and Eike Gebhardt, intro. Paul Piccone (New York, 1978). All citations are from the English translation.

5. Jürgen Habermas, *Theorie des kommunikativen Handelns,* vol. I (Frankfurt, 1981), p. 518.

6. Adorno, *Negative Dialectics,* trans. E. B. Ashton (New York, 1973), p. xx.

7. This ambiguity is elaborated in Louis Althusser, *Lenin and Philosophy and Other Essays,* trans. Ben Brewster (New York, 1971), p. 178f, where he contends that the original Subject is God, who is both man's master and the model for his own allegedly creative subjectivity.

8. Adorno, 'Subject-Object', p. 498.

9. Walter Benjamin, *Charles Baudelaire: a Lyric Poet in the Era of High Capitalism,* trans. Harry Zohn (London, 1973), p. 103.

10. Adorno, 'Subject-Object', pp. 498–9.

11. Adorno, 'The Actuality of Philosophy', *Telos,* 31 (Spring, 1977), p. 131.

12. Adorno, 'Subject-Object', p. 499.

13. Adorno, *Negative Dialectics,* p. 183.

14. For a discussion of its importance for Marcuse, see Martin Jay, 'Anamnestic Totalization: Reflections on Marcuse's Theory of Remembrance', *Theory and Society,* 11, 1 (January 1982).

15. Adorno, 'Subject-Object', p. 499.

16. Adorno, *Negative Dialectics,* p. 374. See also the comments on p. 190 of that book.

17. Adorno, 'Subject-Object', pp. 499–500.

18. Adorno, *Negative Dialectics,* p. 181.

19. Adorno, 'Subject-Object', p. 500.

20. Adorno, 'Introduction', in Adorno *et al., The Positivist*

Dispute in German Sociology, trans Glyn Adey and David Frisby (London, 1976), p. 12. For a general consideration of Adorno's use of the concept of totality, see Martin Jay, *Marxism and Totality: the Adventures of a Concept from Lukács to Habermas* (Berkeley, 1984).

21. Adorno, 'Subject-Object', p. 501.
22. Adorno, 'Introduction', p. 25.
23. Adorno, *Negative Dialectics,* p. 177. Sohn-Rethel's major work is *Intellectual and Manual Labor,* trans. Martin Sohn-Rethel (Atlantic Highland, NJ, 1977).
24. Adorno, *Negative Dialectics,* pp. 177–8.
25. See, for example, Adorno, 'Introduction', p. 34, where he insists that 'despite all the experience of reification, and in the very expression of this experience, critical theory is orientated towards the idea of society as subject, whilst sociology accepts reification . . .'
26. Horkheimer and Adorno, *Dialectic of Enlightenment,* trans. John Cumming (New York, 1972), p. 230. *Verdinglichung* is mistranslated here as 'objectification'.
27. For a good discussion of the redemptive moment in Benjamin's work, see Jürgen Habermas, 'Consciousness-Raising or Redemptive Criticism: the Contemporaneity of Walter Benjamin', *New German Critique,* 17 (Spring, 1979). For a more general consideration of this issue, see Richard Wolin, *Walter Benjamin: an Aesthetic of Redemption* (New York, 1982).
28. Chiasmus entails the inversion of the word order of one clause in another that follows. See the discussion of its importance for Adorno in Rose, p. 13. It might be noted that another prominent Western Marxist, Maurice Merleau-Ponty, also emphasized chiasmus, which derived from the Greek letter chi (X), as an appropriate way to convey dialectical reversal without premature reconciliation. See his discussion in *The Visible and the Invisible: Followed by Working Notes,* ed. Claude Lefort, trans. Alphono Lingis (Evanston, 1968), chap. IV.
29. Adorno, *Über Walter Benjamin* (Frankfurt, 1970), pp. 159–60.
30. Adorno, *Prisms: Cultural Criticism and Society,* trans. Samuel and Shierry Weber (London, 1967), p. 106.
31. Adorno, 'Subject-Object', p. 501.
32. Ibid., p. 502.
33. Ibid., p. 503.
34. See Martin Jay, 'The Frankfurt School's Critique of Mann-

heim and the Sociology of Knowledge', *Telos*, 20 (Summer, 1974).
35. Adorno, 'Subject-Object', p. 504.
36. Adorno, *Prisms*, p. 235.
37. Adorno, 'Subject-Object', p. 505.
38. Idem.
39. Max Horkheimer, *Eclipse of Reason* (New York, 1947); Herbert Marcuse, *Negations: Essays in Critical Theory*, trans. Jeremy J. Shapiro (Boston, 1968).
40. Horkheimer, *Eclipse of Reason*, p. 274.
41. Adorno, 'Subject-Object', p. 506.
42. Idem.
43. Friedemann Grenz, *Adornos Philosophie in Grundbegriffen: Auflösungen einiger Deutungsprobleme* (Frankfurt, 1974), p. 44.
44. Adorno, 'Introduction', p. 58.
45. Benjamin's initial critique of the Kantian notion of scientific experience came in his 'Über das Programm der kommenden Philosophie', originally written in 1918 and first published in Horkheimer, ed., *Zeugnisse. Theodor W. Adorno zum sechzigsten Geburtstag* (Frankfurt, 1963). His distinction between the two types of experience is developed in his *Passagenwerk* fragments, some of which have been collected in *Charles Baudelaire: a Lyric Poet in the Age of High Capitalism*. It was anticipated by Dilthey, although it is not clear that Benjamin was directly influenced by him. See Michael Ermarth, *Wilhelm Dilthey: the Critique of Historical Reason* (Chicago, 1978), p. 226.
46. For Benjamin's treatment of the relationship between narrative and experience, see his 'The Storyteller: Reflections on the Works of Nicolai Leskov', in *Illuminations: Essays and Reflections,* ed. with intro. Hannah Arendt, trans. Harry Zohn (New York, 1968).
47. See, in particular, Benjamin, 'On Language as Such and on the Language of Man' and 'On the Mimetic Faculty', in *Reflections: Essays, Aphorisms, Autobiographical Writings,* ed. with intro. Peter Demetz, trans. Edmund Jephcott (New York, 1978), and 'Doctrine of the Similar', *New German Critique,* 17 (Spring, 1979).
48. Benjamin, 'On Language as Such and on the Language of Man', *Reflections*, p. 318.
49. Adorno, *Negative Dialectics*, p. 376.
50. Adorno, 'The Actuality of Philosophy', p. 127.
51. This phrase of Weber's has been made widely known by

Clifford Geertz's influential version of cultural anthropology. See his *The Interpretation of Cultures* (New York, 1973), p. 5.

52. Paul Ricoeur, *Freud and Philosophy: an Essay on Interpretation,* trans. Dean Savage (New York, 1970), p. 33.
53. Adorno, 'Resignation', *Telos,* 35 (Spring, 1978); see also his remarks in 'Marginalien zu Theorie und Praxis' in *Stichworte.*
54. Adorno, 'Resignation', p. 168.
55. Adorno, 'Subject-Object', p. 510.
56. Idem.
57. Ibid., p. 511.
58. Idem.

3. The Fractured Totality: Society and the Psyche

1. 'For nothing but despair can save us.' Quoted by Adorno in his conversation with Arnold Gelsen, 'Ist die Soziologie eine Wissenschaft vom Menschen?'
2. For an excellent history of the concept of critique, see Paul Connerton, *The Tragedy of Enlightenment: an Essay on the Frankfurt School* (Cambridge, 1980), p. 17f.
3. Author's conversation with Adorno, Frankfurt, March 1969.
4. Adorno's experience as an émigré did, however, make him aware of the importance of bourgeois democracy in a way that he had not been earlier. See, for example, *Minima Moralia: Reflections from Damaged Life,* trans. E. F. N. Jephcott (London, 1978), pp. 112–13.
5. 'Sociology and Psychology', *New Left Review,* 46 (November–December 1967) and 47 (January–February 1968).
6. Ibid., part I, p. 78.
7. Ernst Bloch, *Spuren* (Berlin, 1930). For Adorno's sympathetic appreciation, see his 'Bloch's "Traces": the Philosophy of Kitsch', *New Left Review,* 121 (May–June 1980).
8. *Dialectic of Enlightenment,* trans. John Cumming (New York, 1972), p. 231.
9. *Minima Moralia,* p. 61.
10. Ibid., p. 63.
11. Idem.
12. Ibid., p. 64.

13. Ibid., p. 61.
14. Ibid., p. 49.
15. Ibid., p. 95.
16. 'Die revidierte Psychoanalyse', *Gesammelte Schriften,* VIII (Frankfurt, 1972), p. 32.
17. Letter from Adorno to Benjamin, 2 August 1935, in *New Left Review*, ed., *Aesthetics and Politics: Debates between Bloch, Lukács, Brecht, Benjamin, Adorno,* afterword by Fredric Jameson (London, 1977), p. 113.
18. 'Freudian Theory and the Pattern of Fascist Propaganda', in *The Essential Frankfurt School Reader,* eds. Andrew Arato and Eike Gebhardt, intro. Paul Piccone (New York, 1978), p. 136.
19. Lasch, *Haven in a Heartless World: the Family Besieged* (New York, 1977).
20. *Minima Moralia*, p. 23.
21. Ibid., p. 65.
22. See, for example, Jessica Benjamin, 'The End of Internalization: Adorno's Social Psychology', *Telos,* 32 (Summer, 1977), and Mark Poster, *Critical Theory of the Family* (New York, 1978).
23. 'Sociology and Psychology', part II, p. 84.
24. *Minima Moralia,* p. 46. From arguments like this one, it is clear how much Adorno's image of totalitarianism was based on the Nazi rather than Soviet case, for only in the former instance could this contention be even remotely plausible (and even then, not very). As the rest of the aphorism, which is entitled 'Tough baby', indicates, Adorno is conflating homosexuality with its sado-masochistic version.
25. *Dialectic of Enlightenment,* p. 192f.
26. *Prisms,* p. 129. Adorno also used psychoanalytical categories in his analyses of high culture. See, for example, his attack on the psychotic side of Stravinsky in *Philosophy of Modern Music,* trans. Anne G. Mitchell and Wesley V. Blomster (New York, 1980), p. 167f.
27. 'Freudian Theory and the Pattern of Fascist Propaganda', p. 135.
28. 'Reflexionen über Klassentheorie', *Gesammelte Schriften,* VIII.
29. 'Society', *Salmagundi,* 10–11 (Fall, 1969–Winter, 1970), pp. 149–50. See also the chapter on 'Classes and Strata' in *Introduction to the Sociology of Music,* trans. E. B. Ashton (New York, 1976).
30. 'Spätkapitalismus oder Industriegesellschaft?', *Gesammelte Schriften,* VIII.

31. Cited in ibid., p. 360.
32. 'Society', p. 146.
33. 'Schuld und Abwehr' in Friedrich Pollock, ed., *Gruppenexperiement. Ein Studienbericht* (Frankfurt, 1955) and *Gesammelte Schriften*, IX, 2.
34. 'Introduction', *The Positivist Dispute in German Sociology*, trans. Glyn Adey and David Frisby (London, 1976), pp. 26–7.
35. See, for example, 'Zur gegenwärtigen Stellung der empirischen Sozialforschung in Deutschland', *Gesammelte Schriften*, VIII, p. 481; and 'Sociology and Empirical Research', in *The Positivist Dispute*, p. 74.
36. 'Introduction', p. 33.
37. Ibid., p. 37.
38. 'Sociology and Empirical Research', p. 70.
39. 'On the Logic of the Social Sciences', in *The Positivist Dispute*, p. 106.
40. 'Sociology and Empirical Research', p. 69.
41. 'Introduction', p. 12.
42. Idem.
43. Hans Albert, 'The Myth of Total Reason', in *The Positivist Dispute*.
44. 'Thesen über Bedürfnis', *Gesammelte Schriften,* VIII, p. 396.
45. For Adorno's critical reception of Simmel see 'Henkel, Krug und frühe Erfahrung', in Siegfried Unseld, ed., *Ernst Bloch zu Ehren* (Frankfurt, 1965). For his critique of Mannheim, see 'The Sociology of Knowledge and its Consciousness', *Prisms*.
46. In 1967, he contributed an introduction to the German translation of Durkheim's *Sociology and Philosophy*; reprinted in *Gesammelte Schriften*, VIII, as 'Einleitung zu Emile Durkheim, "Soziologie und Philosophie"'.
47. Ibid., p. 251.
48. See the debates that took place at the fifteenth German Sociological Association Congress in 1964, which are collected in Otto Stammer, ed., *Max Weber and Sociology Today,* trans. Kathleen Morris (New York, 1971). Horkheimer, Habermas and Marcuse made contributions that are included in the volume, but Adorno's, which focused more on Theodor Heuss than Weber, is not. Perhaps his strongest praise for Weber appeared in *Negative Dialectics,* trans. E. B. Ashton (New York, 1973), pp. 164–6.

49. Weber, *The Protestant Ethic and the Spirit of Capitalism,* trans. Talcott Parsons (New York, 1958), p. 181.
50. Adorno to Benjamin, 18 March 1936, in *Aesthetics and Politics,* p. 123.
51. 'Spätkapitalismus oder Industriegesellschaft?', p. 359.
52. *Negative Dialectics,* p. 406. One might, perhaps, argue that Adorno's utopianism was a covert source of his pessimism rather than its antithesis, insofar as it created expectations that an imperfect world could never meet. But this would be to sever it too drastically from the reliance on hope that he, like Bloch, Benjamin, Horkheimer and Marcuse, never relinquished, as this passage demonstrates.
53. 'Society', p. 152.
54. Feher, 'Negative Philosophy of Music: Positive Results', *New German Critique,* 4 (Winter, 1975).
55. 'Modern Music is Growing Old', *The Score,* 18 (December 1956).
56. Peter Bürger, 'Die Vermittlungsproblem in der Kunstsoziologie Adornos', *Materialien zur ästhetischen Theorie Th. W. Adornos Konstruktion der Moderne,* eds. Burkhardt Lindner and W. Martin Lüdke (Frankfurt, 1980).
57. See, for example, Arnold Künzli, *Auflärung und Dialektik. Politische Philosophie von Hobbes bis Adorno* (Freiburg, 1971) and Lucio Colletti, *Marxism and Hegel,* trans. Lawrence Garner (London, 1973).
58. Friedemann Grenz, *Adornos Philosophie in Grundbegriffen* (Frankfurt, 1974), p. 161.
59. *Negative Dialectics*, p. 320.
60. Connerton, p. 114.
61. 'Die Idee der Naturgeschichte', *Gesammelte Schriften,* I (Frankfurt, 1973).
62. This remark from *The Communist Manifesto* serves as the title and guiding metaphor for Marshall Berman's *All That is Solid Melts into Air: the Experience of Modernity* (New York, 1982).
63. 'Reflexionen zur Klassentheorie', p. 376.
64. Habermas, 'The Dialectics of Rationalization, an Interview', *Telos,* 49 (Fall, 1981), p. 8.
65. *Dialectic of Enlightenment,* pp. 224–5.
66. *Minima Moralia,* p. 229. At times, to be sure, he did seem to rely on the irreducibility of some particularity, for example in *Negative Dialectics,* p. 346.

4. Culture as Manipulation; Culture as Redemption

1. 'In that which is called philosophy of art, usually one thing is missing: either philosophy or art.' Intended by Adorno as the epigraph of *Ästhetische theorie*.
2. Raymond Williams, *Keywords: a Vocabulary of Culture and Society* (New York, 1976), p. 76.
3. For an excellent overview of the origin of the contrast, see Norbert Elias, *The Civilizing Process*, vol. I: *The History of Manners*, trans. Edmund Jephcott (New York, 1978).
4. Dieter Schnebel, 'Komposition von Sprache – sprachliche Gestaltung von Musik in Adornos Werk', in *Theodor W. Adorno zum Gedächtnis: Eine Sammlung,* ed. Hermann Schweppenhäuser (Frankfurt, 1971).
5. Adorno, *Quasi una Fantasia: Musikalische Schriften II* (Frankfurt, 1963).
6. Geoffrey H. Hartman, *Criticism in the Wilderness: the Study of Literature Today* (New Haven, 1980), p. 190.
7. Adorno, 'Culture and Administration', *Telos,* 37 (Fall, 1978), pp. 100–1.
8. Adorno, 'Culture Criticism and Society', *Prisms: Cultural Criticism and Society,* trans. Samuel and Shierry Weber (London, 1967), p. 26.
9. Ibid., p. 23.
10. Horkheimer and Adorno, *Dialectic of Enlightenment,* trans. John Cumming (New York, 1972), p. 131.
11. Adorno, *Minima Moralia: Reflections from Damaged Life,* trans. E. F. N. Jephcott (New York, 1978), p. 43.
12. Ibid., p. 44. Translation emended.
13. See the discussion of immanent critique in Michael Ermarth, *Wilhelm Dilthey: the Critique of Historical Reason* (Chicago, 1978) p. 313f.
14. Adorno, 'The Sociology of Knowledge and its Consciousness', *Prisms,* p. 48.
15. Ibid., p. 32.
16. The Frankfurt Institute of Social Research, *Aspects of Sociology,* trans. John Viertel (Boston, 1972), pp. 190–1. Adorno's authorship of this passage is confirmed by its being included in his *Gesammelte Schriften,* VIII (Frankfurt, 1972).
17. Ibid., p. 202.
18. For a suggestive analysis of this aspect of its work, see Raymond Geuss, *The Idea of Critical Theory: Habermas and the Frankfurt School* (Cambridge, 1981), chap. I.

19. Adorno, *Negative Dialectics,* trans. E. B. Ashton (New York, 1973), p. 41.
20. Adorno, *Prisms,* p. 31.
21. For a summary of the episode, written largely from Lazarsfeld's point of view, see David E. Morrison, 'Kultur and Culture: the Case of Theodor W. Adorno and Paul F. Lazarsfeld', *Social Research,* 45, 2 (Summer, 1978).
22. Adorno, 'Thesen zur Kunstsoziologie', *Kölner Zeitschrift für Soziologie und Sozialpsychologie,* 19, 1 (March 1967), p. 91.
23. Adorno, 'The Stars Down to Earth: the *Los Angeles Times* Astrology Column', *Telos,* 19 (Spring, 1974).
24. For Jauss's response, see his 'Negativität und ästhetische Erfahrung: Adornos ästhetische Theorie in der Retrospektive', in *Materialien zur ästhetischen Theorie Theodor W. Adornos Konstruktion der Moderne,* eds. Burkhardt Lindner and W. Martin Lüdke (Frankfurt, 1980).
25. See, for example, Dagmar Barnouw, '"Beute der Pragmatisierung": Adorno und Amerika', in *Die USA und Deutschland: Wechselseitige Spiegelungen in der Literatur der Gegenwart,* ed. Wolfgang Paulsen (Berlin, 1976).
26. Adorno, *In Search of Wagner,* trans. Rodney Livingstone (London, 1981), p. 107.
27. Adorno, *Philosophy of Modern Music,* trans. Anne G. Mitchell and Wesley V. Blomster (New York, 1973), p. 167f.
28. Adorno, 'Culture Industry Reconsidered', *New German Critique,* 6 (Fall, 1975), p. 12.
29. Andreas Huyssen, 'Introduction to Adorno', *New German Critique,* 6 (Fall, 1975), p. 4.
30. For an account of these experiments, see John Willett, *Art and Politics in the Weimar Period: the New Sobriety, 1917–1933* (New York, 1978).
31. Ernst Bloch, *Geist der Utopie* (Munich, 1981).
32. Herbert Marcuse, *An Essay on Liberation* (Boston, 1969), p. 38.
33. Leo Lowenthal, *Literature, Popular Culture and Society* (Palo Alto, Calif., 1961), p. 15f.
34. Horkheimer and Adorno, *Dialectic of Enlightenment,* p. 139.
35. Ibid., p. 140.
36. Adorno, 'On the Fetish Character of Music and the Regression of Listening', *The Essential Frankfurt School Reader,* eds. Andrew Arato and Eike Gebhardt, intro. Paul Piccone (New York, 1978), p. 278.

37. Horkheimer and Adorno, *Dialectic of Enlightenment*, p. 158.
38. See note 36.
39. Horkheimer and Adorno, *Dialectic of Enlightenment*, p. 125.
40. Ibid., p. 152.
41. Adorno, 'Culture and Administration', p. 97.
42. Horkheimer and Adorno, *Dialectic of Enlightenment*, p. 121.
43. Adorno, 'Culture Industry Reconsidered', p 14.
44. The essay can be found in Benjamin, *Illuminations: Essays and Reflections*, ed. with intro. Hannah Arendt, trans. Harry Zohn (New York, 1968). The best accounts of the debate are in Susan Buck-Morss, *The Origin of Negative Dialectics: Theodor W. Adorno, Walter Benjamin, and the Frankfurt Institute* (New York, 1977); Richard Wolin, *Walter Benjamin: an Aesthetic of Redemption* (New York, 1982); and Eugene Lunn, *Marxism and Modernism: an Historical Study of Lukács, Brecht, Benjamin and Adorno* (Berkeley, 1982).
45. Adorno, 'On the Fetish Character of Music', p. 296.
46. Adorno, 'On the Social Situation of Music', *Telos*, 35 (Spring, 1978), p. 145. For an account of the complicated Adorno-Eisler relationship, see Günter Mayer, 'Adorno und Eisler', in *Adorno und die Musik*, ed. Otto Kolleritsch (Graz, 1979).
47. Adorno to Benjamin, 18 March 1936, in *New Left Review*, ed., *Aesthetics and Politics: Debates between Bloch, Lukács, Brecht, Benjamin, Adorno*, afterword by Fredric Jameson (London, 1977), p. 122.
48. Siegfried Kracauer, *Theory of Film: the Redemption of Physical Reality* (London, 1960); for Adorno's critical tribute to Kracauer, see 'Der wunderliche Realist', *Noten zur Literatur III* (Frankfurt, 1965).
49. Horkheimer and Adorno, *Dialectic of Enlightenment*, p. 126.
50. Adorno, *In Search of Wagner*, p. 99.
51. Adorno, 'Transparencies on Film', *New German Critique*, 24–25 (Fall–Winter, 1981–2), with a very useful introduction by Miriam Hansen.
52. Horkheimer and Adorno, *Dialectic of Enlightenment*, p. 143.
53. Adorno, 'Transparencies on Film', p. 202.
54. Ibid., p. 203.
55. Idem.
56. Ibid., pp. 203–4.
57. Adorno, 'Freizeit', *Gesammelte Schriften*, X, 2 (Frankfurt, 1977).

58. Ibid., p. 655.
59. Adorno, 'Culture and Administration', p. 102.
60. Adorno, 'Looking Back on Surrealism', in *The Idea of the Modern in Literature and the Arts*, ed. Irving Howe (New York, 1967), p. 223.
61. Adorno, 'Commitment', in *Aesthetics and Politics*, p. 194.
62. Lunn, *Marxism and Modernism*, pp. 195–8, 261–7.
63. The main texts are translated in *Aesthetics and Politics*.
64. T. Wiesengrund, 'Expressionismus und künstlerische Wahrhaftigkeit: zur Kritik neuer Dichtung', *Die Neue Schaubühne*, 2, 9 (1920).
65. Horkheimer, *Aus der Pubertät: Novellen und Tagebuchblätter* (Munich, 1974).
66. For a discussion of several of them, see Diether de la Motte, 'Adornos musikalische Analysen', in *Adorno und die Musik*.
67. Adorno, *Introduction to the Sociology of Music*, trans. E. B. Ashton (New York, 1976); 'Ideen zur Musiksoziologie', *Klangfiguren* (Frankfurt, 1959). For a short analysis of Adorno's place in the sociology of music, see W. V. Blomster, 'Sociology of Music: Adorno and Beyond', *Telos*, 28 (Summer, 1976).
68. See note 46.
69. Adorno, 'On the Social Situation of Music', p. 163.
70. Lucia Sziborsky, *Adornos Musikphilosophie: Genese, Konstitution, Pädagogische Perspektiven* (Munich, 1979).
71. For a useful overview of the tradition, see Carl Dahlhaus, *Esthetics of Music*, trans. William Austin (Cambridge, Mass., 1982).
72. In 'Alban Berg. Zur Uraufführung des "Wozzeck"', *Musikblätter des Anbruch*, 10 (1925), p. 531, he warned against talking of a Schoenberg 'school', although later, when the term became widely used, he was willing to talk of a second Vienna School. See, for example, *Alban Berg. Der Meister des kleinsten Übergangs, Gesammelte Schriften*, *XIII* (Frankfurt, 1971), p. 324.
73. Adorno, *Alban Berg. Der Meister des kleinsten Übergangs*, p. 361.
74. See the discussion in Heinz-Klaus Metzger, 'Adorno und die Geschichte der musikalischen Avantgarde', in *Adorno und die Musik*, p. 9f.
75. Robert Craft, 'A Bell for Adorno', *Prejudices in Disguise* (New York, 1974), p. 91f.
76. Adorno, *Introduction to the Sociology of Music*, p. 211.

183

Adorno borrowed the metaphor of a monad from Benjamin's *The Origin of German Tragic Drama*, trans. John Osborne (London, 1977).

77. Adorno, *Philosophie der neuen Musik* (Tübingen, 1949), p. 38. The English translation imperfectly renders *Geist* as 'the creative impulse' (p. 33). It means instead the objectifications of past subjectivity in Hegel's sense of a cumulative process of cultural and social development.

78. Adorno, *Introduction to the Sociology of Music*, pp. 56–7.

79. Adorno to Krenek, 30 September 1932, in Theodor W. Adorno and Ernst Krenek, *Briefwechsel*, ed. Wolfgang Rogge (Frankfurt, 1974), p. 35.

80. Adorno, *Introduction to the Sociology of Music*, p. 233.

81. Adorno, 'On the Social Situation of Music', p. 128.

82. Ibid., p. 130.

83. Idem.

84. Ibid., p. 131.

85. Idem.

86. Adorno, *Introduction to the Sociology of Music*, p. 197.

87. Ibid., p. 144.

88. Adorno, 'Ideen zur Musiksoziologie', p. 23.

89. Adorno to Krenek, 30 September 1932, *Briefwechsel*, p. 38.

90. Adorno, 'Music and Technique', *Telos*, 32 (Summer, 1977), p. 83.

91. Idem.

92. The types included the expert, the good listener, the culture consumer, the emotional listener, the resentment listener, the entertainment listener, and the indifferent, unmusical or anti-musical listener. See *Introduction to the Sociology of Music*, chap. I.

93. Ibid., p. 18.

94. Adorno, 'Bach Defended against His Devotees', *Prisms*. Adorno seems to have been entirely indifferent to music before Bach.

95. Ibid., p. 139.

96. Idem.

97. See, for example, Rose Rosengard Subotnik, 'Adorno's Diagnosis of Beethoven's Late Style: Early Symptom of a Fatal Condition', *American Musicological Society Journal*, 29, 2 (Summer, 1976), and Carl Dahlhaus, 'Zu Adornos Beethoven-Kritik', in *Adorno und die Musik*.

98. For a typical exchange, see Robert C. Solomon, 'Beethoven and the Sonata Form', and Maynard Solomon, 'Beethoven and the Enlightenment', in *Telos*, 19 (Spring, 1974).

99. Adorno, *Introduction to the Sociology of Music*, p. 209.
100. Ibid., p. 210.
101. Adorno, 'Spätstil Beethovens', *Moments Musicaux: Neu gedruckte Aufsätze 1928–1962* (Frankfurt, 1964); 'Alienated Masterpiece: the *Missa Solemnis*', *Telos*, 28 (Summer, 1976).
102. Adorno, 'Spätstil Beethovens', p. 17.
103. Adorno, 'Alienated Masterpiece', p. 121.
104. Adorno, 'Lyric Poetry and Society', *Telos*, 20 (Summer, 1974), p. 63. Here Adorno was following Benjamin's argument about Baudelaire. See his *Charles Baudelaire: a Lyric Poet in the Era of High Capitalism*, trans. Harry Zohn (London, 1973).
105. Adorno, 'Alienated Masterpiece', pp. 122–3.
106. Adorno, 'Schubert', *Moments Musicaux*, p. 23.
107. Rose Rosengard Subotnik, 'The Historical Structure: Adorno's "French" Model for the Criticism of Nineteenth-century Music', *Nineteenth-century Music*, 2, 1 (July 1978). The French model to which she refers is that of structuralism, whose static qualities she sees in Adorno's view of music between Beethoven and Schoenberg.
108. Adorno, *Philosophy of Modern Music*, p. 130.
109. See, for example, Adorno, 'Gegängelte Musik', *Dissonanzen: Musik in der verwalteten Welt* (Göttingen, 1964).
110. Adorno, 'Reconciliation under Duress', in *Aesthetics and Politics*, pp. 154–5.
111. See note 26.
112. Horkheimer, 'Egoism and the Freedom Movement', *Telos*, 54 (Winter, 1982–3).
113. Joseph Kerman, *Opera as Drama* (New York, 1956), chap. 7.
114. Adorno, *In Search of Wagner*, p. 31.
115. Ibid., p. 38.
116. Ibid., p. 87.
117. Ibid., p. 37.
118. Ibid., p. 154. (Compare the similar remarks at the end of his essay on Spengler in *Prisms*, p. 72.)
119. Ibid., p. 156.
120. Adorno, *Mahler: Eine musikalische Physiognomik*, *Gesammelte Schriften*, XIII, p. 183.
121. Adorno, *Philosophy of Modern Music*, pp. 35–6.
122. Adorno, 'Glosse über Sibelius', *Impromptus: Zweite Folge neu gedruckter Aufsätze* (Frankfurt, 1968); 'Ad vocem Hindemith: Eine Dokumentation', *Impromptus*; 'Stravinksy and Restoration', in *Philosophy of Modern Music*.

See Erik Tawaststjerna, 'Über Adornos Sibelius-Kritik', and Rudolf Stephan, 'Adorno und Hindemith. Zum Verständnis einer schwierigen Beziehung', in *Adorno und die Musik*; and Alfred Huber, 'Adornos Polemik gegen Strawinsky', *Melos*, 38 (1971); and James L. Marsh, 'Adorno's Critique of Stravinsky', *New German Critique*, 28 (Winter, 1983).

123. One might argue that Mahler's *völkisch* sympathies, being directed at the Hapsburg empire, were themselves very cosmopolitan. See the discussion in William J. McGrath, *Dionysian Art and Populist Politics in Austria* (New Haven, 1974), p. 161.
124. Adorno to Krenek, 30 September 1932, *Briefwechsel*, p. 41.
125. Adorno, 'Der dialektische Komponist', *Impromptus*, p. 44.
126. Adorno, 'Arnold Schoenberg, 1974–1951', *Prisms*, p. 154.
127. For an excellent short account of Schoenberg's achievement, which does not draw on Adorno's analysis, see Charles Rosen, *Arnold Schoenberg* (London, 1975; Princeton, 1981).
128. Adorno, 'On the Social Situation of Music', p. 134.
129. Ibid., p. 135. Adorno's pejorative use of 'expressionistically' here derives from his hostility to the version of Expressionism that claimed to draw on a still powerful subject. His own preference was for the Expressionism that registered the crisis of such a subject.
130. Adorno, 'Zur Zwölftontechnik', *Anbruch*, 11, 7/8 (September–October 1929).
131. Adorno, *Philosophy of Modern Music*, p. 99.
132. Ibid., p. 69.
133. Ibid., p. 124.
134. Adorno, 'Modern Music is Growing Old', *The Score*, 18 (December 1956), p. 22.
135. Ibid., p. 23. Despite Adorno's criticism, Boulez contributed a poem entitled 'en marge de la, d'une disparation' to *Theodor W. Adorno zum Gedächtnis*.
136. Thomas Mann, *Doctor Faustus: the Life of the German Composer Adrian Leverkühn as Told by a Friend*, trans. H. T. Lowe-Porter (New York, 1968), p. 478.
137. In *Introduction to Sociology of Music*, Adorno makes a passing reference to *Aida* and *La Traviata*, which, along with Bizet's *Carmen*, he claims 'once meant humanity, the protest of passion against conventional congealment' (p. 87), but this is an isolated remark with no specific historical significance. Adorno, interestingly, never wrote about

Simone Boccanegra, one of whose main characters bears his name.

138. Adorno, *Philosophy of Modern Music*, p. 133.
139. For a description of the episode, see W. Martin Lüdke, *Anmerkungen zu einer 'Logik des Zerfalls': Adorno-Beckett* (Frankfurt, 1981), p. 7.
140. Adorno, 'Lyric Poetry and Society', pp. 57–8.
141. Adorno, 'Ideen zur Musiksoziologie', p. 17.
142. Benjamin, 'On the Mimetic Faculty', *Reflections: Essays, Aphorisms, Autobiographical Writings*, ed. with intro. Peter Demetz, trans. Edmund Jephcott (New York, 1978); 'Doctrine of the Similar', *New German Critique*, 17 (Spring, 1979).
143. Adorno, *Ästhetische Theorie, Gesammelte Schriften, VII* (Frankfurt, 1970), p. 32. The best short account of it in English is Richard Wolin, 'The De-ästheticization of Art: On Adorno's *Ästhetische Theorie*', *Telos*, 41 (Fall, 1979).
144. Adorno, *Philosophy of Modern Music*, p. 217.
145. Adorno, *Ästhetische Theorie*, p. 74f.
146. Ibid., pp. 262–3. Here his reliance on music as the model of the work of art is most obvious.
147. Adorno, 'Modern Music is Growing Old', p. 29.
148. Adorno, *Negative Dialectics*, pp. 17–18.
149. Adorno, 'Culture and Administration', p. 101.

Conclusion

1. 'impatiently patient/in the name of the unteachable/teaching.' Hans Magnus Enzensberger, 'Schwierige Arbeit (für Theodor W. Adorno)' in *Blindenschrift*.
2. Susan Buck-Morss, *The Origin of Negative Dialectics: Theodor W. Adorno, Walter Benjamin, and the Frankfurt Institute* (New York, 1977), pp. 189–90.
3. Irving Wohlfahrt, 'Hibernation: On the Tenth Anniversary of Adorno's Death', *Modern Language Notes*, 94, 5 (December 1979), p. 979.
4. Rose Rosengard Subotnik, 'Why is Adorno's Music Criticism the Way It is? Some Reflections on Twentieth-century Criticism of Nineteenth-century Music', *Musical Newsletter*, 7, 4 (Fall, 1977), p. 11.
5. Adorno, 'On the Social Situation of Music', *Telos*, 35 (Spring, 1978), p. 132.

Short Bibliography

Adorno's *Gesammelte Schriften*, edited by Rolf Tiedemann, began to be published in 1970 by the Suhrkamp Verlag and will include twenty-three volumes when it is completed:

I   *Philosophische Frühschriften* (1973)
II   *Kierkegaard: Konstruktion des Ästhetischen* (1979)
III   *Dialektik der Aufklärung* (1981)
IV   *Minima Moralia* (1980)
V   *Zur Metakritik der Erkenntnistheorie; Drei Studien zu Hegel* (1971)
VI   *Negative Dialektik; Jargon der Eigentlichkeit* (1973)
VII   *Ästhetische Theorie* (1970)
VIII   *Soziologische Schriften I* (1972)
IX   *Soziologische Schriften II*, 2 vols. (1975)
X   *Prismen; Ohne Leitbild; Eingriffe; Kritische Modelle; Stichworte*, 2 vols. (1977)
XI   *Noten zur Literatur* (1974)
XII   *Philosophie der neuen Musik* (1975)
XIII   *Die musikalischen Monographien: Wagner, Mahler, Berg* (1971)
XIV   *Dissonanzen: Einleitung in die Musiksoziologie* (1973)
XV   *Komposition für den Film; Der getreue Korrepetitor* (1975)
XVI   *Klangfiguren; Quasi una Fantasia; Moments Musicaux; Impromptus* (1978)
XVII   *Musikalische Schriften IV* (1982)
XVIII   *Musikalische Schriften V* (in preparation)
XIX   *Musikalische Schriften VI* (in preparation)
XX   *Miszellan* (in preparation)
XXI   *Fragmente I: Beethoven* (in preparation)
XXII   *Fragmente II: Theorie der musikalischen Reproduktion* (in preparation)
XXIII   *Fragmente III: Current of Music* (in preparation)

Short Bibliography

SELECTIONS FROM ADORNO'S CORRESPONDENCE

Theodor W. Adorno and Ernst Krenek, *Briefwechsel,* ed. Wolfgang Rogge (Frankfurt, 1974)
Theodor W. Adorno, *Über Walter Benjamin* (Frankfurt, 1970)

BOOKS OF ADORNO AVAILABLE IN ENGLISH

Aesthetic Theory, trans C. Lenhardt (London, forthcoming)
Against Epistemology: a Metacritique, trans. Willis Domingo (Oxford, 1982; Cambridge, Mass., 1983)
Composing for the Films, with Hanns Eisler (New York, 1947); appeared only under Eisler's name until published in Germany in 1969
Dialectic of Enlightenment, with Max Horkheimer, trans. John Cumming (New York, 1972; London, 1973)
In Search of Wagner, trans. Rodney Livingstone (London, 1981)
Introduction to the Sociology of Music, trans. E. B. Ashton (New York, 1976)
The Jargon of Authenticity, trans. Knut Tarnowski and Frederic Will (London, 1973)
Minima Moralia: Reflections from Damaged Life, trans. E. F. N. Jephcott (London, 1974)
Negative Dialectics, trans. E. B. Ashton (New York and London, 1973)
Philosophy of Modern Music, trans. Anne G. Mitchell and Wesley V. Blomster (New York and London, 1973)
Prisms: Cultural Criticism and Society, trans. Samuel and Shierry Weber (London, 1967)

BOOKS IN ENGLISH CONTAINING EXTENSIVE SECTIONS BY ADORNO

Aesthetics and Politics: Debates between Bloch, Lukács, Brecht, Benjamin, Adorno, ed. *New Left Review,* afterword by Fredric Jameson (London, 1977)
Aspects of Sociology, by The Frankfurt Institute of Social Research, trans. John Viertel (Boston, 1972; London, 1973)
The Authoritarian Personality, by Adorno *et al.* (New York, 1950)
The Essential Frankfurt School Reader, eds. Andrew Arato and Eike Gebhardt, intro. Paul Piccone (New York and Oxford, 1978)

Adorno

The Intellectual Migration: Europe and America, 1930–1960, eds. Donald Fleming and Bernard Bailyn (Cambridge, Mass., 1969)
The Positivist Dispute in German Sociology, Adorno *et al.,* trans. Glyn Adey and David Frisby (London, 1976)

WORKS ON ADORNO

Beier, Christel, *Zum Verhältnis von Gesellschaftstheorie und Erkenntnistheorie. Untersuchungen zum Totalitätsbegriff in der kritischen Theorie Adornos* (Frankfurt, 1977)
Buck-Morss, Susan, *The Origin of Negative Dialectics: Theodor W. Adorno, Walter Benjamin, and the Frankfurt Institute* (New York, 1977)
Grenz, Friedemann, *Adornos Philosophie in Grundbegriffen: Auflösung einiger Deutungsprobleme* (Frankfurt, 1974)
Jimenez, Marc, *Theodor W. Adorno: art, idéologie et théorie de l'art* (Paris, 1973)
Kolleritsch, Otto, ed., *Adorno und die Musik* (Graz, 1979)
Lindner, Burkhardt and Lüdke, W. Martin, eds., *Materialien zur ästhetischen Theorie Theodor W. Adornos Konstruktion der Moderne* (Frankfurt, 1980); contains extensive annotated bibliography of items on Adorno from 1969 to 1979
Lüdke, W. Martin, *Anmerkungen zu einer 'Logik des Zerfalls': Adorno-Beckett* (Frankfurt, 1981)
Nebuloni, Roberto, *Dialettica e storia in Theodor W. Adorno* (Milan, 1978)
Oppens, Kurt *et al., Über Theodor W. Adorno* (Frankfurt, 1968)
Pettazzi, Carlo, *Th. Wiesengrund Adorno: Linee di origine e di sviluppo del pensiero (1903–1949)* (Florence, 1979); contains a full bibliography of items from the extensive Italian reception of Adorno
Rose, Gillian, *The Melancholy Science: an Introduction to the Thought of Theodor W. Adorno* (New York and London, 1978)
Sauerland, Karol, *Einführung in die Ästhetik Adornos* (Berlin, 1979)
Schoeller, Wilfried F., ed., *Die neue Linke nach Adorno* (Munich, 1969)
Schweppenhäuser, Hermann, ed., *Theodor W. Adorno zum Gedächtnis* (Frankfurt, 1971)
Sziborsky, Lucia, *Adornos Musikphilosophie: Genese, Konstitution, Pädagogische Perspektiven* (Munich, 1979)

190

Short Bibliography

von Friedeburg, Ludwig and Habermas, Jürgen, eds., *Adorno-Konferenz 1983* (Frankfurt, 1983); excellent bibliography complied by René Görtzen.
Zuidervaart, Lambert, *Refractions: Truth in Adorno's Aesthetic Theory* (PhD, University of Amsterdam, 1981)

WORKS WITH EXTENSIVE SECTIONS DEVOTED TO ADORNO

Jameson, Fredric, *Marxism and Form: Twentieth-century Dialectical Theories of Literature* (Princeton, 1971)
Jay, Martin, *Marxism and Totality: the Adventures of a Concept from Lukács to Habermas* (Berkeley, 1984)
Lunn, Eugene, *Marxism and Modernism: an Historical Study of Lukács, Brecht, Benjamin and Adorno* (Berkeley, 1982)
Rosen, Michael, *Hegel's Dialectic and Its Criticism* (Cambridge, 1982)
Wolin, Richard, *Walter Benjamin: an Aesthetic of Redemption* (New York, 1982)

SPECIAL ISSUES OF JOURNALS DEVOTED TO ADORNO

Utopia (Milan, 1972)
Studia Philosophica Gandensia (Meppel, 1972)
Text + Kritik (Munich, 1977)
Humanities in Review, 2, 4 (Los Angeles, 1979)

GENERAL WORKS ON THE FRANKFURT SCHOOL

Apergi, Francesco, *Marxismo e ricerca sociale nella Scuola di Francoforte (1932–1950)* (Florence, 1977)
Bonss, Wolfgang and Honneth, Axel, eds., *Sozialforschung als Kritik: Zum sozialwissenschaftlichen Potential der Kritischen Theorie* (Frankfurt, 1982)
Connerton, Paul, *The Tragedy of Enlightenment: an Essay on the Frankfurt School* (Cambridge, 1980)
Dubiel, Helmut, *Wissenschaftsorganisation und politische Erfahrung: Studien zur frühen Kritischen Theorie* (Frankfurt, 1978)
Friedman, George, *The Political Philosophy of the Frankfurt School* (Ithaca, 1980)
Geuss, Raymond, *The Idea of a Critical Theory: Habermas and the Frankfurt School* (Cambridge, 1981)

Adorno

Held, David, *Introduction to Critical Theory: Horkheimer to Habermas* (Berkeley and London, 1980)

Jay, Martin, *The Dialectical Imagination: a History of the Frankfurt School and the Institute of Social Research, 1923–1950* (Boston, 1973; London, 1973)

O'Neill, John, ed., *On Critical Theory* (New York, 1976; London, 1977)

Rusconi, Gian Enrico, *La teoria critica della società* (Bologna, 1968)

Slater, Phil, *Origin and Significance of the Frankfurt School: a Marxist Perspective* (London, 1977)

Söllner, Alfons, *Geschichte und Herrschaft: Studien zur materialistischen Sozialwissenschaft, 1929–1942* (Frankfurt, 1979)

Tar, Zoltan, *The Frankfurt School: the Critical Theories of Max Horkheimer and Theodor W. Adorno* (New York and Chichester, 1977)

There are many articles on Adorno and the Frankfurt School, as well as translations of various Frankfurt School essays, in the journals *Telos*, *New German Critique* and *New Left Review*. See also the special issue of *Esprit*, 17, (5 May 1978).

Index

193

Index

Index

Kierkegaard, Søren, 29, 30, 32, 35, 52, 70, 75, 158
Kirchheimer, Otto, 44
Klossowski, Pierre, 21
Kluge, Alexander, 127
Kolakowski, Leszek, 53, 56
Korsch, Karl, 15, 16, 53, 85
Kracauer, Siegfried, 11, 14, 25–26, 28, 43, 87, 120, 126
Kraus, Karl, 28, 151
Krenek, Ernst, 27, 135, 138, 150
Kürnberger, Ferdinand, 24

Lacan, Jacques, 85
Language, 75–77, 156
Lasch, Christopher, 92
Lazarsfeld, Paul, 34, 39, 45, 118
Le Bon, Gustave, 91
Lefebvre, Henri, 84
Leibniz, Gottfried von, 133
Leiris, Michel, 21
Lenin, Vladimir I., 26
Levinson, Daniel, 39
Loos, Adolf, 151
Lourié, Arthur, 41
Lovejoy, Arthur, 13
Lowenthal, Leo, 13, 16, 28, 44, 46, 121–122
Löwy, Michael, 18
Ludendorff, Erich, 52
Lukács, Georg, 18, 22, 57, 63, 66, 68–69, 74, 87, 88, 100, 129–130, 136, 145, 146, 153; Hegelian Marxism and, 20, 29, 35, 43, 48, 64, 73, 75, 105–106; Western Marxism and, 14–16, 53, 59, 84–85
Lunn, Eugene, 130

Mach, Ernst, 26
Mahler, Gustav, 149
Mallarmé, Stéphane, 126

Mann, Thomas, 17, 18, 25, 41, 111, 152
Mannheim, Karl, 48, 71, 101, 116
Marcuse, Herbert, 18, 29, 33, 38, 46, 48, 68, 84, 85, 93; Frankfurt School and, 16, 44, 47, 72, 120
Marx, Karl, 29, 36, 37, 38, 45, 48, 56, 57, 59, 78, 83, 85, 89, 95, 107, 114, 122, 146; exchange principle and, 66–67
Marxism, 15–16, 28–29, 33, 47, 56, 59, 66–68, 71, 80, 95–96, 124; Marxist aesthetics, 129, 146; Marxist economics, 82–84. See also Western Marxism; Hegelian Marxism
Materialism, 18, 113
McCloy, John J., 44
Mitscherlich, Alexander, 46
Mitscherlich, Margarete, 46
Modernism, 17, 108, 129–130. See also Aesthetic modernism
Montaigne, Michel de, 121
Mozart, Wolfgang Amadeus, 141
Music, 131–158; as commodity, 136, 147; critical possibilities in, 136–137, 152; composer's role in, 137–138; jazz, 119–120, 123; 'New Music,' 27, 40–42, 106, 131–140, 150–154; reproduction of, 138–139; society and, 133–149, 153; tonality in, 134, 149, 150–153. See also 'Second Viennese School'

Napoleon Bonaparte, 143
Nazism, 116
Neue Sachlichkeit, 129, 130

197

Index

Neumann, Franz, 44, 46
New Left, 47, 55, 161
Nietzsche, Friedrich, 37, 42, 65, 78, 85, 96, 114, 119, 132, 147; deconstructionism and, 22, 108–109; exchange principle and, 68–59
Nominalism, 80, 97

Ohnesorg, Benno, 154
Oxford University, 32–33

Parsons, Talcott, 87, 98
Pascal, Blaise, 121
Patti, Adelina, 25
Phenomenology, 26, 32–33, 70–71
Pilot, Harald, 51
Plato, 156
Polanyi, Karl, 82
Pollock, Friedrich, 16, 34–36, 44
Popper, Karl, 12, 51, 74, 96
Positivism, 32, 51, 58, 62, 69
Protagoras, 89
Proust, Marcel, 101
Psychoanalysis, 19, 26, 29, 85, 87; Adorno and, 39–40, 45–46, 89–94
Psychology, 87–89, 93–94, 132, 150–151
Pult und Taktstock, 27, 135

Rationality, 132, 138, 152; instrumental reason, 17, 37, 102–103, 107, 141; Vernunft, 30, 37, 72–73; Verstand, 72–73, 97
Reductionism, 71–72
Reich, Wilhelm, 85, 93
Reification, see Adorno, on reification
Restoration, 143

Ricoeur, Paul, 78
Rimbaud, Arthur, 106
Risorgimento, 153
Rockefeller Foundation, 34, 42
Romanticism, 17, 141, 146, 158; anti-capitalism and, 18
Rosenzweig, Franz, 20
Rottweiler, Hektor (pseudonym for Adorno), 33
Russian Revolution, 83

Sado-masochism, 33, 41, 93, 153
Sanford, R. Nevitt, 39
Sartre, Jean-Paul, 130, 154
Saussure, Ferdinand de, 76
Scheinwerfer, Der, 135
Schlegel, Friedrich, 111
Schleiermacher, Friedrich, 116
Schlöndorff, Volker, 127
Schoenberg, Arnold, 11, 27–28, 40–42, 48, 101, 106, 131–134, 140, 150–153, 154, 161, 163
Scholem, Gershom, 19, 49
Schopenhauer, Arthur, 29, 132
Schubert, Franz, 145
Science, 38, 51, 107
'Second Viennese School,' 16, 27–28
Secularization, 141
Sekles, Berhard, 25
Sibelius, Jean, 149
Silbermann, Alphons, 118, 132
Simmel, Georg, 84, 101, 102
Socialism, 16
Sociology, 50–51, 83–84, 87, 96–98, 100–104
Sohn-Rethel, Afred, 67
Soviet Union, 29, 120, 153
Spengler, Oswald, 17, 18, 35, 48
Spiritualism, 30
Stendhal, 110

198